CU00751347

UNDERCURRENTS

Farm Incomes:
Myths and Reality

UNDERCURRENTS

Other titles in the series

UNDERCURRENTS   Series Editor Carol Coulter

Farm Incomes: Myths and Reality

ALAN MATTHEWS

CORK UNIVERSITY PRESS

First published in 2000 by
Cork University Press
University College
Cork
Ireland

©Alan Matthews 2000

All rights reserved. No part of this book may be reprinted
or reproduced or utilized in any electronic, mechanical or other
means, now known or hereafter invented, including photocopying and
recording or otherwise, without either the prior written permission
of the Publishers or a licence permitting restricted copying in
Ireland issued by the Irish Copyright Licensing Agency Ltd,
The Irish Writers' Centre, 19 Parnell Square, Dublin 1.

British Library Cataloguing in Publication Data
A CIP catalogue record for this book is available from
the British Library

ISBN 1 85918 241 0

Typeset by Tower Books, Ballincollig, Co. Cork
Printed by ColourBooks Ltd., Baldoyle, Co. Dublin.

Contents

Acknowledgements

I am very grateful to Brendan Kearney, Dermot McAleese, Deirdre O'Connor and Aidan O'Driscoll for information and very useful comments on an earlier draft of the book. The views expressed and any remaining errors are entirely my own responsibility.

Alan Matthews,
March, 2000

If we are to do something about the significant number of farmers whose incomes have suffered dramatically because of the appalling weather conditions, we should take some of the £1 billion in direct aid which is going to farmers who are successful, commercial and rich. They should be told that they can survive in a competitive economy and a significant proportion should be transferred, particularly money which is being paid for set aside in tillage, in income subsidies to those parts of the farming community which are genuinely suffering. Let us have a redistribution within agriculture instead of the eternal obsession with a redistribution from those not in agriculture to those in agriculture.
Senator B. Ryan, Seanad Debates, 14 October 1998.

Having listened to Senator Ryan, I hope he never becomes Minister for Agriculture and Food. As bad as the present Minister is regarded by the farmers, Senator Ryan would be a total disaster. He has no concept of farming or the farming way of life. We are trying to preserve a culture and a way of life. Agriculture is not an exact science like physics or chemistry; it is different.
Senator E. Caffrey, Seanad Debates, 14 October 1998.

The meager and paltry fodder scheme top up of £150 offered by the Minister to some affected farmers is an insult. It is totally insignificant and it would hardly buy a few tonnes of feed. At a minimum, farmers should have been able to lay their hands on between £4,000 and £5,000, preferably interest free or, if not, at a low rate of interest, to help tide them over.
Senator D. Coghlan, Seanad Debates, 10 February 1999.

Something must be done and I call on the Minister as a minimum response to ensure that the equivalent of the proceeds of the sale of the ACC, which we are given to believe will be about £200 million, is earmarked to help address the serious structural problems in agriculture and in rural Ireland.
Senator A. Doyle, Seanad Debates, 10 February 1999.

The ACC, through the State, has supported farmers and kept them going. The ACC owes farmers nothing; it is farmers, if anything, who owe the ACC a debt of gratitude over a number of decades. To suggest now that the proceeds should go to those who have already been the subject of ACC munificence, is really gilding the lily. It is saying to farmers that, because they are so used to being subsidised by the ACC, we are going to sell the ACC and give them the proceeds. This is utterly absurd.
Senator S. Ross, Seanad Debates, 10 February 1999.

They got virtually everything for which they asked, but now they want more. They are like Oliver Twist.
Mr D. Ahern, Minister for Social, Community and Family Affairs, Select Committee on Social, Community and Family Affairs, 10 March 1999, referring to farmers' reaction to the new Farm Assist scheme.

Introduction

The autumn and winter of 1998 were a difficult time for farmers in Ireland. Prices for cattle, sheep and pig farmers, in particular, collapsed in the second half of the year. Unfavourable weather and problems in the Russian meat market – the extent and nature of which were not anticipated – were the primary causes. Aggregate farm income, according to Central Statistics Office figures, fell by 5 per cent in 1998 compared to the previous year. The wet weather led to a fodder crisis particularly in the West of Ireland. In Brussels, discussions were taking place on the EU commission's Agenda 2000 proposals for further reform of the Common Agricultural Policy. The commission had proposed only partial compensation for the reductions in support prices for arable, beef and dairy products and the detailed proposals appeared biased against the extensive grassland farming typical of this country. The Irish Farmers' Association predicted further income losses of £260 million per annum if the proposals were implemented and redundancy for 50,000 farmers within five years. The contrast between the bleak farming outlook and the booming Celtic Tiger in the rest of the economy in the winter of 1998 could not have been starker.

The government was not unmindful of the difficulties facing farmers and a series of measures was introduced to ease their situation. They included increased export refunds for beef and pigmeat, the introduction of aids to private storage for sheep and pigmeat, improved access to intervention for heavier cattle, an increased rate of advance payment of suckler cow and special beef premia, the speeding up of payments to farmers, approval of additional shipping capacity for livestock export and the introduction in December of a special fodder package of £21 million, including £12 million in fodder payments, £6 million for mountain ewe destocking and almost £3 million in sheep headage top-up. In February 1999 the Minister of Agriculture and Food, Mr Joe Walsh, announced a further £20 million in fodder aid for farmers, bringing the total government contribution to £41 million. The government also announced in the 1999 budget the new Farm Assist income-support scheme designed to assist farmers with income difficulties.

It is clear from the quotations preceding this introduction (taken from parliamentary debates on the 1998 farm income situation) that not all were in agreement with what the government should do. On the one hand, there were those who felt not enough was being done and that farmers deserved more help. On the other hand, there were those who argued that farmers already benefited from substantial income transfers and that the crisis could be alleviated by a more targeted distribution of these transfers.

These differing viewpoints suggest there is a need to distinguish fact from fiction where farm incomes are concerned. The politics of farm incomes are easily muddied by claim and counter-claim based on the use and misuse of statistics. One objective of this book is to clarify the factual basis for the measurement of farm incomes and agricultural support. Is there still a farm-income problem? How do farm incomes compare on average to non-farm incomes? How important is public support to the sector? Who gets this support? What would happen if public support was reduced or removed? This book examines these issues in the context of the ongoing debate on the future of agricultural policy.

The first schemes of agricultural price support were introduced in Ireland during the 1930s as part of Fianna Fail's economic policy to promote greater agricultural self-sufficiency and to assist farmers adversely affected by the so-called Land War with Britain. Prior to that, the Cumann na nGael government had had little time for direct aids to agriculture in the form of subsidies or guaranteed prices. It argued that in a mainly agricultural country the cost of such assistance would be paid for the most part by the agricultural community itself. Market intervention to support farm incomes was extended in the 1950s and 1960s at a time when Irish agriculture was almost completely dependent on the British market. This market was open to imports from any source and fierce competition led to very low prices. British farmers were protected from the worst consequences of this competition (which, of course, kept food prices low to British consumers) by a system of direct payments. Under the 1965 Anglo-Irish Free Trade Agreement, these payments were partially extended to Irish producers by the UK Exchequer in return for conceding free trade in industrial products with the United Kingdom.

Farmers were in favour of EU membership in the early 1970s (or the European Economic Community as it was then called) as it appeared to promise an unlimited market for agricultural produce at prices well above what they were getting at the time. The high prices were the result of the protectionist Common Agricultural Policy. This was an integral part of the EU's founding Treaty of Rome as a result of a mutual bargain between France and Germany. France gained access to the high-price German food market in return for opening up its domestic market to German industrial goods. Not for the last time in EU negotiations, Irish farmers were able to benefit from a deal struck by France in the pursuit of its domestic farm agenda.

It is widely perceived that Ireland has benefited from the Common Agricultural Policy (CAP). Despite occasional income crises caused by fluctuations in farm prices or weather conditions, there is no longer a generalised farm income problem. Although the return to labour employed in agriculture remains lower than in the non-farm sector because of differences in age and education levels, the total income of farm households now exceeds average household income in the state. The risk of poverty among farmers has fallen dramatically (although it has not been eliminated) and the quality of life in rural areas has been vastly improved. It is not only farmers who benefited. Supporters of the CAP point to the fact that Ireland is unique among EU member states in the size of the transfers it receives as a result of its operation, amounting to about 4 per cent of Irish GNP.

In 1992, a reform of EU agricultural policy (known as the MacSharry reform after the EU Agriculture Commissioner Ray MacSharry who was responsible for its implementation) changed its direction radically. The substance of this reform was the substitution of direct payments to farmers for part of the traditional market price support. While its immediate impact was to increase the budgetary cost of the Common Agricultural Policy, MacSharry simultaneously introduced a ceiling on these payments which ensured greater control of agricultural policy expenditure over time. Further steps in the same direction were taken as part of the EU Agenda 2000 agreement reached in Berlin in May 1999.

This book argues that more could and should have been done to reform the CAP at that time. Despite the apparent benefits from an Irish perspective, EU agricultural policy has become increasingly indefensible. It is incredible that today the entire income from farming comes from public subsidies from Irish and EU taxpayers and consumers. Not only that, but the cost of providing this support now greatly exceeds the actual income received by farmers. Increasingly, these costs are being picked up by Irish taxpayers and consumers, while the benefits accrue disproportionately to larger farmers. Structural change in the agricultural industry means that fewer and fewer farmers are the beneficiaries of the CAP's largesse. The generalised farm income problem of a generation ago has disappeared, but this has more to do with the improved education of farm people, the greater opportunities for off-farm employment and more generous social welfare assistance to elderly farmers than with agricultural policy as such. The traditional defences of the CAP, even from an Irish point of view, are no longer convincing in the light of reality.

This book challenges a number of myths about Irish farming and farm incomes:
- that agriculture plays a key productive role in the economy as a strong natural resource-based sector. In reality, farming in Ireland is now justified primarily by its success in harvesting premia and other EU supports. If outputs and inputs are measured at world prices, the business of producing farm commodities makes a negligible contribution to Irish GNP. Farming is profitable only because of the enormous transfers it receives

as a result of public policy. The book develops a new method of calculating agriculture's contribution to Irish GNP which disentangles the subsidy aspects in the official figures.

- that agriculture as a sector contains a disproportionate number of low income households and is therefore a justified recipient of public support. In reality, farm household incomes are now at least as high as non-farm incomes, and the incidence of farm poverty is lower than in the economy as a whole.
- that the bulk of farm support is paid for by the EU and thus that the direction of agricultural policy is of little concern to Irish taxpayers and consumers. In reality, the burden of farm support on Irish taxpayers and consumers now amounts to over £900m annually or half of income from farming and it is likely to grow over time. The cost to Irish consumers alone is equivalent to a VAT of 20 per cent on food.
- that EU agricultural payments to Ireland represent a significant transfer to the Irish economy and benefit not just farmers but also the economy as a whole. In reality, the inefficiencies associated with this transfer greatly reduce their value. As a society, we would be better off with a different orientation of agricultural policy.

Two aspects of EU agricultural policy are singled out for particular criticism. The first is the system of market price support whereby farmers are paid above world market prices at the expense of consumers in Ireland and elsewhere in the EU. The second is the way that direct payments to farmers are coupled to production leading to a skewed distribution of these payments and unnecessary additional costs in the payment of support. The argument is also made that overall economic welfare could be improved by a radical reform of EU policy which would see farmers producing at world prices while maintaining budget transfers for agri-environment and rural development purposes.

Of course, a change of this magnitude would have to be managed with care. Farmers should continue to receive support to move out of agriculture into non-agricultural activities. To protect the viability of rural areas, policies focusing particularly on strengthening the town and village network and creating off-farm employment opportunities should be pursued. The 1999 White Paper on Rural Development and the National Development Plan point the way forward, although as long as agricultural policy grabs the lion's share of resources, rural development will remain a Cinderella activity. With virtually full employment in the non-agricultural sector, it makes sense to embark on a change of this kind at this time.

Grasping this opportunity will require a sea-change in political attitudes at home as well as the forging of new alliances within the EU. While the next round of agricultural trade liberalisation got off to a poor start following the failure of the Seattle WTO ministerial meeting in December 1999 to agree an agenda, there is agreement to press ahead with negotiations over the next few years. This provides an opportunity to open up again the future of EU agricultural policy. Instead of siding with the protectionist forces inside the EU on this occasion, Ireland should use the opportunity to seek a mutual 'disarmament' of agricultural protectionism on both sides of the Atlantic and beyond on a phased basis. Embracing the opportunity to re-orient agricultural policy along market lines would lead to a healthier agricultural sector and a more sustainable basis for the continued growth of the Irish economy into the new millenium.

1. Income trends in farming

This chapter sets the scene for the discussion of farm income by showing how income from farming is measured and how it has changed over time. Preliminary estimates of aggregate income from farming are made by the Central Statistics Office, Dublin, in December of each year and subsequently revised and confirmed as additional data become available. Publication is an eagerly awaited event, and the figure is highlighted and discussed by the farm organisations and politicians as an indicator of farming's economic health. However, there are a number of different measures of farm income, each of which may be useful in its own way. The relationship between these measures is illustrated in Table 1.1.

The income account begins with the revenue that farmers receive for selling their crops and livestock called the *gross output* of agriculture. Information is collected from meat factories, creameries, grain merchants and other traders on the value of cattle, milk, sheep, cereals and other farm outputs purchased from farmers. On the input side, the equivalent figure is intermediate consumption or *total input*, which is the sum of all the items purchased by farmers from other sectors of the economy

TABLE 1.1: The income account:
relationship between measures of farm income.

	1973	1980	1990	1995	1998
Gross agricultural output	621.4	1,710.8	3,226.7	3,573.0	3,260.2
Less total input of materials and services	195.8	760.0	1,351.1	1,653.2	1,760.5
Gross agricultural product at market prices	425.6	950.8	1,875.6	1,919.9	1,499.6
Less depreciation	39.6	186.1	337.0	378.9	461.3
Net agricultural product at market prices	**386.0**	**764.7**	**1,538.6**	**1,541.0**	**1,038.3**
Plus subsidies	20.2	52.4	382.9	747.5	1,038.0
Less agricultural levies	15.4	60.3	52.3	36.3	24.9
Net agricultural product at factor cost (i.e. income arising in agriculture)	**390.8**	**756.8**	**1,869.2**	**2,252.3**	**2,051.5**
Less wages, salaries and land annuities	34.6	85.3	166.1	182.0	196.3
Income from self-employment and other trading income	356.2	671.5	1,703.2	2,069.3	1,855.2
Less interest	n.a.	n.a.	246.0	164.4	191.0
Net farm income	**n.a.**	**n.a.**	**1,457.2**	**1,904.9**	**1,664.2**

Source: Department of Agriculture and Food, *Compendium of Irish Economic and Agricultural Statistics* and *Annual Review and Outlook*, various years.

and which are used up within a farming year, such as processed feedstuffs, fertiliser, fuel and veterinary services.

Subtracting total input from gross output gives *gross agricultural product* or *gross value added* at market prices. Subtracting depreciation on machinery and buildings yields *net agricultural product* or *net value added* at market prices. This item is normally an indicator of a sector's productive contribution to the overall economy but can be highly misleading in the case of agriculture, as discussed more fully in Chapter 7.

To arrive at the actual income earned from agricultural activity, an adjustment is required to take account of direct subsidies (less levies) linked to production. In national accounting terms, this is equivalent to moving from a measure of value added at market prices to a measure of value added at factor cost. Net agricultural product at factor cost is equivalent to agriculture's share in national income in the national income accounts. It is more widely known as *income arising in agriculture* and is the first income indicator used in farm income discussions.

A second indicator, *income from self-employment in agriculture*, is the income concept most used in Ireland. It is a measure of the amount available to pay farm family workers for their labour and management and to pay a return on own and borrowed capital. It is derived from income arising in agriculture by subtracting payments to hired labour and payments of land annuities.

A third indicator, *net farm income*, is only available since 1980 when official estimates of interest paid were first published. It measures the return to farmers' labour, management and own capital. It is derived from income from self-employment in agriculture by subtracting interest paid on borrowed capital. One of the problems in making this estimate is distinguishing between farmers' interest payments on borrowings for business and for personal purposes, which are often drawn on the same account.

In each case, these series must be deflated in order to get their value in real terms. Possible price deflators which can be used for this purpose include the Consumer Price Index (CPI) and the implicit price index of gross domestic product at market prices (the GDP deflator). The latter deflator is the best measure of changes in the value of money over time due to inflation and thus gives a measure of agricultural income in constant prices. The practice in Ireland is to use the CPI deflator and the resulting series is then a measure of changes in the purchasing power of income from agricultural activity over time.

The trend in income from self-employment in agriculture in real terms is shown in Fig. 1.1. EU membership commenced in 1973, and Irish agricultural statistics often take that year as their starting point. But because of the inherent volatility of many agricultural statistical series, the choice of a base year can influence the interpretation of the observed trend. This is particularly clear in the income series in Fig. 1.1. Between 1970 and 1973 there was

FIG 1.1: Aggregate income from farming,
1970–98, constant 1998 prices.

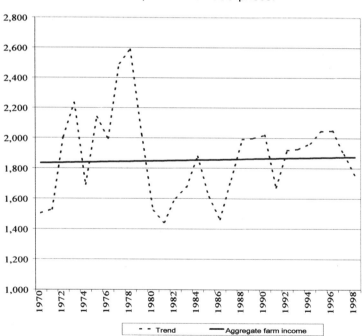

Source: Estimated Output, Input and Income in Agriculture, December/July various years, CSO.

a sharp increase in the real value of income from self-employment in agriculture. This took place partly because of anticipation of the effects of EU entry but also because of very buoyant world markets around that time. The year 1973 was thus a peak one for aggregate farm income, exceeded only by the two years 1977 and 1978 during the past thirty years. If 1973 is taken as the starting point, Fig. 1.1 suggests that income from agriculture has tended to decline over this period. Starting from 1970, which is a more representative year in relation to the income experience of the 1960s, suggests on the contrary a slightly increasing trend over time.

Whichever year is chosen as the base year, the most striking characteristic of aggregate income from farming is its volatility. The peak 1973 figure was followed by a sharp fall in 1974, only to recover over the next five years to reach a new peak in 1978. This was followed by a dramatic collapse over the next three years as farmers suffered an acute price-cost squeeze following Irish entry into the European Monetary System (EMS). Prior to then, high Irish inflation had been offset by a steady devaluation of the Irish pound. With EMS entry, the authorities tried to maintain the value of the Irish pound but failed to control inflation, and as a result farming was plunged into its most severe income crisis less than ten years after EU membership. Since then, aggregate income has recovered, but with significant falls again in 1985–6 and in 1990–1. The sharp recovery in 1987 was helped by the 1986 devaluation of the Irish pound. Poor world commodity markets, the first BSE crisis in Britain and the outbreak of the Gulf War caused the downturn in 1990–1.

Incomes quickly recovered, however, in the years 1994 through 1996. This period coincided with the phasing-in of the MacSharry CAP reforms, which the farming organisations had predicted would be catastrophic for Irish farming. The fact that they turned out to be good years for farming was partly fortuitous. Direct payments were increased to compensate for a fall in market support prices. But market prices during this period, particularly for arable crops, did not fall; in fact, they strengthened because world prices hit a peak at this time. The EU even introduced export taxes on wheat in 1995 and 1996 in order to try to keep down the EU price, it was getting so high. Yet farmers still received the increased direct payments intended to compensate them for a fall in prices. From an Irish perspective, the value of the payments in Irish pounds was further increased due to the Irish pound devaluation in 1993. At the same time, the devaluation also mitigated the fall in support prices which the payments were intended to compensate.

Not surprisingly, aggregate income from farming in 1996 was higher in real terms than at any time since the previous peak in 1979. It is against this background that the fall in income in 1997 and 1998 should be judged. Aggregate income in 1998 was 14 per cent below the 1996 level in real terms, and 7 per cent below trend. Further, in a crisis it is rare that all sectors of farming are hit to the same degree. Dairy farming, in particular, continued to be very profitable in both 1997 and 1998 and the fall in income felt by the remaining sectors in farming was proportionately greater.

It is clear that aggregate farm income has experienced sudden jumps and collapses throughout the period of EU membership. Individual farmers experienced even greater volatility because of the averaging that occurs in aggregating individual incomes to the national level. It is important that both farmers themselves and policy-makers acknowledge that incomes can be volatile and plan accordingly. The drop in aggregate farm income between 1996 and 1998 was less severe than had occurred on four previous occasions in the past thirty years (1974, 1981, 1986 and 1991). Yet farming organisations and policy-makers continue to seek emergency solutions to each new crisis instead of providing effective risk-management and income-insurance schemes. In any reform of agricultural policy this should be an important priority.

The other important characteristic of aggregate income from farming is the growing contribution of direct subsidies. Direct subsidies are defined as non-capital payments made directly to farmers. They include headage (cattle and sheep), premia (cattle, sheep and extensification), arable aid, disease-eradication schemes, certain forestry premia, installation aid for young farmers and payment under the Rural Environment Protection Scheme. They now amount to a staggering £1 billion annually and constitute a vital part of farm income. They contributed 56 per cent of aggregate farm income in 1998, compared to 22 per cent in 1991. Given their importance, the next chapter describes the operation of these schemes in more detail.

2. How farm incomes are supported

The individual farmer must accept the going market price and has no influence over the price received for the produce he or she has to sell. However, the market for agricultural products is far from being a free market. It is, for many agricultural products, a tightly controlled market protected by trade barriers against lower-priced imports and supported by government subsidies to exports and, ultimately, a government guarantee to purchase at a minimum price if no other buyers can be found at that price. Although product prices can and do fluctuate in response to market forces, the prices farmers are paid are by and large *administered* prices. They are set by the EU Council of Agricultural Ministers who, of course, are responsive to the pressures from their farming lobbies at home. So, although individual farmers cannot influence the market price, organised farmers have a very powerful influence on agricultural product prices within the EU.

The EU in 1992 introduced a significant change in farm-price support. This was in response to its growing cost and the need to ensure the ability to continue to make transfers to farmers in the context of the likely outcome of the Uruguay Round of trade negotiations. These trade negotiations, under the auspices of GATT, the General Agreement on Tarriffs and Trade, concluded in 1993 with an agreement to put limits on certain types of agricultural support while permitting countries to provide support which did not have a distorting effect on trade. From a virtually exclusive reliance on making transfers to farmers through market mechanisms by keeping market prices artificially high, the EU embarked on a partial substitution of market price support by direct payments to farmers. Some direct-payment schemes have been introduced for social reasons, some for environmental, and some are to mitigate the impact of reductions in product prices which are supported by CAP commodity regimes. Direct payments have thus grown in importance and, as noted in Chapter 1, made up 56 per cent of aggregate farm income in Ireland in 1998. Under the Agenda 2000 agreement in May 1999, this policy is set to continue and direct payments will become an even more important source of farm income in future.

This chapter explains the mechanisms used to support farm prices and farm incomes in the European Union. EU support policies and transfers are financed from the EU's agricultural budget which goes under the initials FEOGA. This is an abbreviation of the French version of the English title European Agricultural Guarantee and Guidance Fund. The title indicates that there are two parts to the FEOGA budget. The first part, called the Guarantee Section, is intended mainly to finance the cost of market-support operations. The second part, called the Guidance Section, is intended to finance socio-structural operations. These include schemes to assist the modernisation of farming, to facilitate adjustments in farm structures and to promote rural development. Guidance Section expenditure in Ireland is treated as part of the EU Structural Funds. Structural Fund expenditure is administered through multi-annual operational programmes approved by the EU Commission as part of the EU's Community Support Framework agreed with the Irish government.

Transfers to farmers are made under a bewildering variety of schemes, each with its own administrative conditions, financing and operational procedures. The more important arrangements include market-price support, premia payments, headage payments, payments under the CAP accompanying measures, socio-structural aids, community initiatives and national measures. The purpose of this chapter is to briefly chart a path through this territory.

Market price support

The purpose of EU market price support is to ensure that farmers receive a higher price than they would do if they had to face unrestricted competition from the rest of the world. To make sure that this happens, the EU restricts import access, pays subsidies on exports and supports the domestic market through intervention-buying and aids to private storage. Since the WTO Agricultural Agreement came into force on 1 January 1995 there have been significant changes in the way in which these protection mechanisms work.

Before 1 January 1995 import protection was provided by means of variable levies. The EU fixed a minimum import price for each commodity, and imposed a variable levy equal to the difference between this minimum import price and the lowest offer price from a third country competitor. If a competitor tried to overcome this import barrier by lowering its price, the EU simply increased the size of the variable levy in response. This system had two effects. First, it ensured that imports could only enter the EU if the EU market price was above the minimum import price, thus protecting EU farmers against more competitive world market suppliers. If world prices exceeded EU domestic prices, the variable levy system could be reversed and export taxes imposed to keep the EU domestic price stable as a gesture to EU consumers. Second, it protected EU farmers and consumers against fluctuations in world market prices which could not be transmitted to the EU domestic market. A consequence of this policy was to intensify world market price fluctuations to the detriment of, for example, poorer developing countries who have no choice but to import or export at the prevailing world prices.

As part of the WTO agreement variable levies were replaced by fixed tariffs. The EU generally chose to implement tariffs as absolute amounts rather than in percentage terms. Thus the tariffs are proportionately higher when world prices are low, and vice versa, preserving some of the stabilising function of the former variable levies. However, the most important point about the tariffs is their size. Compared with tariffs on industrial goods which now average 3–4 per cent in the EU and rarely exceed 20 per cent for particularly sensitive commodities such as textiles, agricultural tariffs are enormous. They range from 50–90 per cent for cereals, 70–90 per cent for dairy products and 168 per cent for sugar. Under the WTO agreement these tariffs must be reduced by an average of 30 per cent over the six years to 2000 but even with this reduction they provide significant protection against third country imports.

Import protection is sufficient to raise internal prices if the EU is a net importer of an agricultural commodity. For most products the EU is now an exporter and so must pay export subsidies to maintain internal prices higher than world prices. Prior to 1 January 1995 export subsidies could be paid at whatever level was necessary to clear the market, subject only to the necessary budget finance being available. Since the WTO agreement took effect, the EU's freedom of manoeuvre is limited in two respects. First, there are specific limits on the volume of exports each year which can be subsidised and second, there are limits on the overall expenditure on export subsidies by commodity by year.

Export subsidies are particularly important to Ireland's beef and dairy exports to third countries outside the EU. The profitability of, for example, live cattle exports to the Middle East or beef sales to Russia are very dependent on the level of export subsidy offered. Export subsidies for each commodity are administered by an EU management committee composed of senior agricultural officials from each member state. Tenders for specified volumes of exports are sought from exporters in the EU. Because of relatively buoyant world commodity markets since the WTO agreement entered force, the WTO restrictions on the use of export subsidies have not proved binding until now.

If Irish cattle prices are depressed, as they were in the autumn and winter of 1998, then Ireland can seek to have the size of tenders and the amount of export subsidy increased, particularly on categories of live cattle and beef and to markets of greatest interest to Ireland. The subsidy is paid to the exporting firm, not directly to the farmer. It is hoped that competition between firms who have secured a tender will ensure that the subsidy benefits are passed back in the form of higher prices to suppliers. Among Irish meat factories, in particular, competition appears relatively ineffective and the Minister of Agriculture and Food complained on many occasions in the Dail that the export subsidy increase he secured in the winter of 1998 on behalf of beef farmers was not reflected in the prices that factories paid. This is one example of the way in which benefits intended for farmers may be captured by other players in the agro-food chain.

As the final defence against low prices, the EU can remove surplus produce from the EU market either through intervention purchases or aids to private storage. Both mechanisms are essentially holding operations intended to deal with temporary situations of over-supply. If the EU market remains in surplus, then supplies in intervention must eventually be disposed of outside the EU with the aid of export subsidies. Intervention was an important outlet for Irish beef cattle throughout the 1980s and the system was hugely costly to the EU budget. One of the objectives of the MacSharry CAP reforms was to reduce reliance on intervention and to make it more of a support system of last resort.

To this end, the EU has lowered the guaranteed price for so-called safety-net intervention for cattle and made the criteria for acceptance of products into intervention more stringent. For example, intervention for beef cattle prior to October 1998 was restricted to male cattle in certain quality grades and with a carcases weight less than 340kg, which meant that only about 15 per cent of the Irish national steer kill was eligible for intervention. One of the measures sought by the Minister for Agriculture and Food to alleviate the 1998 fall in farm incomes was increased access to intervention for heavier cattle. Following Irish representations, the carcass weight limit was increased from 340kg to

360kg and the steer 04 category also became eligible. Both these measures allowed for close to 50 per cent of our steer production to become eligible for intervention. If the WTO restraints on export subsidies become binding in any year, intervention is an important safeguard to prevent farm prices from collapsing.

Premium schemes

The CAP reform measures, which became effective on 1 January 1993, switched the emphasis in the support system in the case of the beef and arable sectors away from intervention-purchasing towards direct payments to farmers under the Livestock Premium and Arable Aid Schemes. Support to sheep farmers always took the form of a direct payment since the introduction of the common sheepmeat regime in 1980 and this has continued.

There are half a dozen different livestock premium schemes from which farmers can benefit. They include the special beef premium paid on male animals twice in their lifetime; a suckler cow premium paid on suckler cows; a bull premium scheme paid on bulls; a calf processing scheme to encourage the slaughter of calves; while ewes are eligible for a variable premium depending on the difference between a guaranteed price for lamb and the actual market price.

The 1992 reform introduced quota arrangements for the Livestock Premium Schemes (individual quotas in the case of the suckler cow and ewe premium schemes and a national quota in the case of the special beef premium scheme). Where individual quotas are in place, farmers who keep greater numbers of stock are not eligible for additional premia. Given the importance of these premia to the overall profitability of livestock rearing, few farmers would find it worthwhile to exceed their individual quotas. However, the transfer/leasing of quotas is permitted between farmers and there are ewe premium and suckler cow premium national reserves from which farmers, who fulfil certain criteria, may draw. In the case of the special beef premium scheme, the value of the premium paid is reduced if the total number of applications from farmers exceeds the national quota although to date this has not occurred.

Stocking-density limits were also introduced to encourage extensive farming. This involves the payment of an extensification premium on suckler cows and male bovine animals already paid their respective suckler cow and special beef premium grants on holdings with low stocking levels (less than 1.4 livestock unit/ha). Where a producer's stocking density is less than 1.0 livestock unit/ha, a further extensification premium is paid. In addition, a deseasonalisation slaughter premium for male cattle is paid to encourage more even slaughtering patterns throughout the year.

Headage schemes

Premium schemes are the basic form of direct payment to livestock producers, but they are supplemented in areas of the country that qualify as disadvantaged by additional headage support. Fully 75 per cent of the total country is now designated as disadvantaged for headage payment purposes, with different payment schemes applying depending on the severity of disadvantage. The total payment a farmer may receive is subject to various limits. For example, only the first sixty livestock units on a holding qualify for full rate of grant, with livestock units in excess of sixty qualifying for payment at half rate. Payments are limited to £89.62 per forage hectare for beef cows, sheep, goats and equines paid at full rate, and to £55.99 per forage hectare for all cattle other than beef cows, paid at full rate, and to 1.4 livestock units per forage hectare, whichever is lesser. There is an overall limit of £4,000 in combined headage payments. If the regulations appear complex, they are. They prioritise grantsmanship over stockmanship. Rewarding the paperwork skills needed to maximise grant payments rather than the management skills to produce good stock is just one small example of the way agricultural policy undermines the efficiency of agricultural production.

And the rewards are substantial. For the fairly large beef

TABLE 2.1: Example of direct payments
support on a beef farm, 1998.

Scheme	Payment rates	Payment
Special beef premium		
10-month premium	25 x £85.61	£2,140.25
22-month premium	25 x £85.61	£2,140.25
Suckler cow premium	50 x £133.14	£6,657.00
Basic Direct Payments		**£10,937.50**
Spring slaughter premium (if operating)	25 x £34.24	£856.00
Extensification premiums (if stocking below 1.4 livestock units/ha)		
10-month	25 x £28.35	£708.75
22-month	25 x £28.35	£708.75
Suckler cow (if stocking below 1.0 livestock unit/ha)	50 x £28.35	£1,417.50
10-month	25 x £69.30	£1,732.50
22-month	25 x £69.30	£1,732.50
Suckler cow	50 x £69.30	£3,465.00
Additional Payments (if all apply and at maximum rate)		**£7,786.00**
Total Basic & Additional Payments		**£18,723.50**
Headage Payments if in Disadvantaged Areas		
More Severely Handicapped Areas		
Beef cow payments	40 cows x 84.00	£3,360.00
Total headage if More Severely Handicapped		£3,360.00
Reps Payment	40ha x £118.90	**£4,760**
Total Possible Payment		**£26,840**

This example outlines the benefits in direct payments and headage payments based on the 1999 values of the premia for a drystock farmer with fifty suckler cows rearing all calves to slaughter stage. It assumes that twenty-five bullocks are sold as finished animals.

Source: Modified from ICOS, *CAP Reform: Guide to the New CAP Measures*.

farmer shown in Table 2.1, for example, if he or she is able to draw down all the available benefits, his or her income from government payments alone would amount to almost £27,000. In addition, of course, he has whatever income he can earn from the sale of the cattle themselves. Unfortunately, National Farm Survey statistics show that, on average, beef farmers just about cover their costs from market revenue, so that the direct payments de facto are their sole source of income. It is an alarming state of affairs when cattle farming, the mainstay of Irish agriculture for the past 150 years, can no longer even cover its costs under the Common Agricultural Policy.

Arable aids

Arable farmers are also included in a direct payments scheme. Under the support system for producers of arable crops arising from the 1992 CAP reform, producers of cereals, oilseeds and protein crops are entitled to claim direct area-related payments to compensate them for the reductions in market support prices. Participation in the support system is not compulsory but, if a producer wants to receive compensatory payments, he or she must join the system and may have to set-aside land. The land a producer uses to claim area payments and set-aside payments must meet certain conditions in relation to past use. The deliberate idling of good agricultural land is another example of how agricultural policy undermines production efficiency.

Claims can be submitted under either of two schemes. The General Scheme applies to larger producers, i.e. those with more than 15.13 hectares (ha) under cereals. Under this scheme, applicants can be required to set aside a minimum percentage of their land. The obligatory rate of set aside for the 1999 harvest was fixed at 10 per cent. Producers may set aside an additional 10 per cent above the obligatory rate on a voluntary basis, i.e. a total of 20 per cent. The Simplified Scheme applies to smaller producers, i.e. those with less than 15.13ha under cereals. There is no set-aside requirement under this scheme. On average, cereal growers in the general scheme had around 50ha of cereals and would be entitled to around £13,000 each at 1999 rates of payment.

From the records of the Department of Agriculture and Food it is possible to estimate the distribution of compensation and headage payments by size of payment. The 1994 distribution is shown in Table 2.2. Around 70 per cent of the recipients of the smallest amounts shared 30 per cent of the total between them, while around 3 per cent of recipients received around 25 per cent of the total. Just 146 farmers received over £100,000 each in direct payments in that year.

Accompanying measures

The 1992 CAP reform opened up a number of other new channels of direct payments to farmers in addition to compensatory payments and headage payments. The Rural Environment Protection Scheme (REPS) is one of the three accompanying measures to CAP Reform, the others being an early retirement scheme and an afforestation scheme. The objectives of the scheme are laudable. They are to establish farming practices that reflect the increasing public concern for conservation, landscape protection and wider environmental problems; to protect wildlife habitats and endangered species of flora and fauna; and to produce quality food in an extensive and environmentally friendly manner. Under REPS, a participant farmer is required to draw up a waste storage, management, liming and fertilisation plan for his or her farm and a grassland management plan for

TABLE 2.2: Headage, Premia and Arable
aid payments, 1994.

Category	No. of payees	Per cent of total recipients	Per cent of total payments (est.)
Less than £2,000	55,169	40	8
£2,000 to £5,000	46,214	33	22
£5,000 to £10,000	34,240	25	47
£10,000 to £50,000	2,160	2	10
£50,000 to £100,000	1,322	1	13
£100,000 or greater	146	0.1	2
Total No. of Payees	139,281	100	100
Total amount of payments	£701.3m		

Source: Parliamentary Question no. 75, Thursday, 16 May, 1996 by Opposition (FF) spokesperson for Agriculture (Mr. B. Cowen TD) to Minister for Agriculture, Food and Forestry (Mr I. Yates). *Column 4 is based on the author's estimates.*

his or her farm that avoids overgrazing and poaching of land. Farmers in REPS are paid a basic premium of 151 euros (approximately £119) per hectare up to a maximum of 40ha. Farmers with land area in excess of 40 hectares must implement REPS measures on all their lands. REPS payments are annual for a five-year period. The scheme also provides for additional payments to scheme participants who undertake one or more of the scheme's supplementary measures such as preserving Natural Heritage Areas, organic farming or the rearing of animals of local breeds in danger of extinction. By the end of 1999, almost 43,000 farmers were in REPS with an expenditure of £173 million in that year.

No one can criticise the objectives of REPS. The question is whether the scheme provides value for money. A full evaluation of the scheme was undertaken during 1999 and its conclusions will make interesting reading. Casual observation suggests that the additional environmental benefits obtained from the expenditure of £170 million annually are small in that the payments are going to farmers who have to make minimal if any adjustments to their farming behaviour. If this is the case, then the scheme has functioned more as an income support than an environmental scheme. Perhaps this does not matter very much, as the scheme to date has been funded 75 per cent by the EU and only 25 per cent from the national exchequer. So on cost-benefit grounds it makes sense to try to maximise the uptake of the scheme and not worry too much about its environmental impact.

Under the afforestation scheme generous premiums are paid to farmers to encourage the planting of trees. However, the introduction of REPS has made many farmers think twice about putting land into forestry and the rate of forest-planting has dropped dramatically since REPS came on line. Already, there are calls for further increases in the forestry grants to help make forestry more competitive. Landowners can play off one land use against the other to extract greater and greater hectare aids and the hapless taxpayer is left wondering where the catch is.

TABLE 2.3: Direct income payments and
leview in agriculture, 1993–98.

	1993	1994	1995	1996	1997	1998
	Payments (£m)					
Headage	80.8	136.6	118.0	116.2	126.4	123.3
of which						
Cattle headage	52.3	93.8	80.2	81.4	88.8	87.6
Beef cow	10.3	19.0	17.0	11.3	13.4	12.5
Sheep headage	18.2	20.8	20.4	22.5	23.9	22.6
Livestock premia, compensation packages and arable aid	292.8	458.8	547.4	672.9	620.6	711.2
of which						
Suckler cow	62.3	89.9	112.2	157.7	121.3	176.7
Special beef premium	48.3	122.5	169.8	167.1	157.8	198.0
Deseasonalisation premium	8.6	15.6	15	16.8	23.8	26.4
Ewe premium	128.6	117.3	108	113.2	73.6	94.2
Extensification premium	-	47.5	59.8	60.5	66.9	80.1
Special BSE compensation				69.0	31.2	7.6
Agri-monetary compensation					50.4	16.3
Arable aid	45.0	66.0	82.5	88.6	95.7	94.5
Other schemes						
of which						
Fodder scheme 1998						12.1
Cull ewe scheme						5.3
Disease eradication schemes including BSE slaughtering	19.1	17.2	20.9	28.9	34.4	36.6
Milk payments	21.4	36.6	18.4	17.3	38.9	14.3
Forestry payments	-	1.0	4.2	12.6	10.9	16.4
Installation aid for young farmers	2.6	2.3	4.2	6.5	7.0	3.4
Rural environment protection scheme	-	1.2	30.9	56.4	101.4	132.8
Others	6.3	15.8	4.0	0.7	0.8	0.0
Total Payments	**422.9**	**669.5**	**747.5**	**911.4**	**940.4**	**1,038.0**
	Levies (£m)					
Bovine disease eradication	28.8	28.0	28.8	13.2	10.1	8.1
Superlevy			4.0	14.0	7.9	10.6
Others (including co-responsibility levies)	12.8	3.8	3.5	3.5	5.1	6.2
Total Levies	**41.6**	**31.8**	**36.3**	**30.5**	**23.1**	**24.9**
Payments less Levies	0.7	9.1	5.8	878.9	917.3	1,013.1

Source: Department of Agriculture and Food.

Expenditure on direct payment schemes

Overall expenditure on direct payment schemes is shown in Table 2.3. Although the 1992 CAP reform was introduced from 1 January 1993, the additional payments to farmers under this reform did not actually begin until 1994. The impact of the reform is shown by the more than doubling of direct payments between 1993 and 1996 when the reforms were completed. Payments reached a record level of over £1 billion in 1998 partly because efforts were made to accelerate payments to assist farm incomes in that year. The Special Beef Premia, the Suckler Cow Premium, headage payments and REPS payments between them account for the bulk of direct payment expenditure. The growth of REPS payments over this period is particularly noteworthy. Set against the total of more than £1 billion in direct payments in 1998, the fodder aid scheme worth £12 million could clearly make only a limited impact.

Socio-structural aids

Payments are also made to farmers under socio-structural schemes. These are of a different nature to the direct payment schemes discussed above in that they are mostly irregular capital payments to farmers. In Ireland, socio-structural aid has been channelled to farmers through the Operational Programme for Agriculture, Rural Development and Forestry 1994–99. The 1994–99 Programme, which was the second of its type, emphasised support for the following areas: general structural improvement, including on-farm capital investment; farm diversification; compensatory allowances; forestry; the environment; and research, advisory services and training. Total public funding of over £1,285m, including EU funding of £738m, was made available for the six-year period.

These expenditures are justified on the economic grounds that they are intended to improve farm efficiency and productivity, rather than on the social grounds used to justify income transfers. However, an Economic and Social Research Institute

(ESRI) evaluation of the socio-structural schemes funded by the EU Structural Funds in the 1994–99 period found that most agricultural expenditure was distributional rather than productive in nature. Either farmers were being paid to undertake investment which they were obliged to do but may not have been able to afford (dairy hygiene and pollution-control schemes) or farmers were being paid to undertake investment which they would have been prepared to do even in the absence of aid (in which case the scheme is simply transferring public money to farmers with no overall national gain). Thus socio-structural expenditure must be added to market price support and direct payment schemes when computing the size of the public transfer to farming.

This chapter has described the main schemes under which income transfers to farmers currently take place. They fall into three main categories: market price support schemes, direct payment schemes and socio-structural aids. While the details of the individual schemes can be bewildering, and in any case change from year to year, over £1 billion annually is now paid to farmers in direct payments alone under a variety of justifications. But a full accounting of the support to agriculture must also take account of the value of market price support. Estimating the value of market price support raises its own tangled web of issues. The next chapter takes up the challenge of estimating total support paid to farmers and compares it to aggregate income from farming. The results we shall see are startling.

3. The importance of farm subsidies to farm income

The previous chapter described the mechanisms that transfer income to farmers. The three main categories are market price support schemes, direct payments and socio-structural aids. This chapter asks how important is this support relative to the total income from farming. It shows that farm income is now totally dependent on the transfers received from EU and Irish taxpayers and consumers. Farmers, once pillars of enterprise, have become as dependent on the state for their income as any social welfare recipient. While the purpose of social welfare payments is to alleviate poverty, however, the purpose of farm payments is less clear.

Measuring farm support

Since the early 1980s there has been substantial interest in measuring and comparing the size of the support provided to agriculture across countries. This work was pioneered by the Paris-based Organisation for Economic Co-operation and Development (OECD) during the run-up to the Uruguay Round negotiations on agricultural trade liberalisation. The OECD developed an indicator of agricultural transfers which was initially called the Producer Subsidy Equivalent (PSE). Since 1998, this measure has been redefined and is now called the Producer Support Estimate (with the same PSE acronym). The PSE measures assistance to producers as the value of transfers from domestic consumers and taxpayers to producers resulting from a given set of agricultural policies (an equivalent Consumer Subsidy Equivalent [CSE] measures the transfers to and from consumers alone). It is a comprehensive indicator of support, taking into account both market price support and budgetary transfers (including direct payments and input subsidies). The OECD does not consider the purpose of payments made to farmers; all payments are counted, including agri-environment payments. Both indicators are published annually for the OECD members (including the EU as a single entity). Using these data it is possible to make comparisons between countries on a reasonably harmonised basis.

Figure 3.1 shows that the value of transfers to EU farmers (measured in nominal terms) has continued to increase over the past ten years and currently runs at ECU 116 billion annually. However, as a proportion of EU GDP, it has fallen from 2·3 per cent in 1986–88 to 1·4 per cent in 1998. In order to get a

FIG 3.1: EU Producer support estimates, 1986–98.

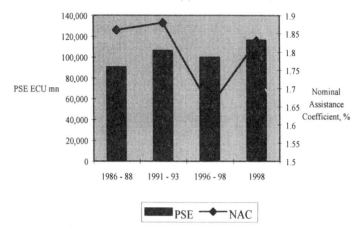

Source: OECD, *Agricultural Policies in OECD Countries: Monitoring and Evaluation 1999*, Paris.

sense of the scale of these numbers, it is useful to look at two ratios. One is to express the value of PSE transfers as a percentage of the value of agricultural output (measured at the supported prices which producers actually receive and including the value of direct payments to them). The resulting *percentage PSE* is a relative measure of the importance of agricultural support in total agricultural revenues. The EU figure has varied between 30 per cent (in the early 1980s) to 45 per cent (in the mid-1980s). It dipped below 40 per cent in the mid-1990s but increased again to 45 per cent in 1998. Changes in the percentage PSE are mostly due to changes in world prices relative to internal EU prices and thus in the value of the market price support component of the PSE. During periods of high world prices (such as the mid-1990s), the apparent protection provided to EU farmers declines and the value of support measured by the PSE falls, and vice versa.

The second ratio measures the value of support in terms of the degree of protection farmers receive compared to world prices. It is called the *Nominal Assistance Coefficient* and is the ratio of the effective price obtained by farmers in the EU (the market price plus the average value of direct payments) compared to the world price level. The trend in this ratio is shown by the continuous line in Fig. 3.1. The figure of 1.86 in the mid-1980s means that, on average, the effective price of agricultural products for EU farmers was 86 per cent higher than observed world price levels. The OECD calculates Nominal Assistance Coefficient values of 2.32 for milk, 2.61 for beef and a whopping 2.84 for sheepmeat in 1998. This means that, in that year, effective sheep prices in the EU were nearly three times the world market level. These figures are indicative of the way in which farmers in the EU are protected against the chill winds of competition from lower-cost producers elsewhere in the world.

Market price support

The major component of the Producer Support Estimate for the EU is market price support, accounting for ECU 72 billion of the ECU 116 billion of support in 1998. As noted above, the size of this component depends on the gap between the EU internal market price and the world market price. The presumption is being made that, in the absence of support, these are the prices which EU farmers, including Irish farmers, would receive.

It is often argued that existing world prices are residual or dumping prices because they apply only to the limited volumes of farm produce which are sold on world markets and that fewer farmers are expected to produce at these prices. The point being made is that it is unreasonable to use these prices as a benchmark against which to measure support to farmers. World prices are indeed depressed because of the extensive agricultural protection in nearly all industrialised countries. As a result, for some commodities little is traded at world prices. The EU is a big player on world markets, and any change in EU production or consumption as a result of removing price support would impact on world prices. Further, if CAP reform took place in the context of a multilateral agreement to liberalise agricultural trade, such that support was simultaneously removed also for US, Japanese and other exporters, world prices might be very different to what they are today. Simulation models suggest that the increases could be in the range 5–30 per cent, with lower figures applying to grains and higher figures applying to livestock and particularly dairy products.

Faced with this problem of trying to determine an appropriate world price benchmark against which to measure the value of support to Irish farmers, there are three alternatives:

1. the first is to use actual world prices as the OECD has done, often based on the prices received by competitor countries. Comparison with producer prices in other countries shows that EU prices are well above those in other major exporters. For example, in 1996 when the EU price for R3 bullocks/steers was 2,679 ECU/tonne carcases weight, the US price was 1,779 ECU/tonne, the Australian price was 1,238 ECU/tonne and the Argentinian price was 1,202 ECU/tonne. This method has the virtue of using observed prices but they are likely to over-estimate the real value of support because they do not take into account the dumping nature of these prices. The use of actual world prices as a benchmark against which to measure the value of market price support is called here the OECD method.

2. the second is to try to come up with reasonable estimates of what world prices would be in the *absence* of support. The Department of Agriculture and Food has made some estimates of what Irish producers would obtain in the absence of the CAP in recent years. For beef, they estimate Irish prices are some 50–55 per cent higher, for dairy products some 14–40 per cent higher. The implicit price gaps are clearly smaller than the OECD figures, even allowing for the fact that the OECD nominal assistance coefficient includes the value of direct payments as well as market price support.

3. a third approach is to derive 'implicit' world prices by taking the value of the export subsidy which the EU pays on exports from the EU and subtracting this from the producer price paid to farmers. As the export refund is meant to bridge the gap

between internal and world prices, it could be argued that the world price derived in this way is what Irish farmers would receive if the EU had to eliminate these export subsidies. This approach gives much higher estimates of the value of support than even the OECD method. For example, the Minister for Agriculture and Food told the Dail in October 1998 that the export refund provided to meat exporters to allow them trade in markets outside the EU would amount to 51p per pound on male carcass beef. At the time, the highest price being paid for cattle was 80p per pound. If a 51p subsidy is included in that price, then the beef is being sold to third countries for 29p per pound. Not all beef sold benefits from a subsidy of this magnitude, but it is indicative of the gap that currently exists between EU and world prices.

The value of support to farmers

Deirdre O'Connor of University College Dublin has estimated the value of support received by Irish farmers using the OECD method of deriving world prices. Her results for recent years are shown in Table 3.1. They take into account market price support, direct payments and socio-structural aids but not the general services that benefit farmers collectively. Both EU and national expenditure is included. The market support element is based on world price gaps calculated by taking the difference between Irish producer prices and the world reference prices used by the OECD in its calculation of the EU Producer Support Estimates.

Some doubts about the appropriateness of the OECD world price benchmarks are raised when we observe that the support figures for pig and poultry producers in the table are negative. While this partly reflects the fact that pig and poultry farmers are penalised by a support policy which raises the price of grains and thus animal feed, it also reflects the fact that Irish producer prices for pigs and poultry are below the world reference price used by the OECD. As there is no policy reason why Irish pig and poultry exports should get less than the world price, this suggests that

TABLE 3.1: Agricultural support in relation to income
from farming, 1995–97.

Producer Support Estimate (£m)	1995	1996	1997
Beef	957	985	902
Sheepmeat	191	213	149
Pigmeat	26	29	-15
Poultrymeat	7	-3	-7
Wheat	38	20	21
Barley	89	73	72
Milk	729	600	568
Total PSE, selected commodities	2,037	1,917	1,690
Memo items			
Income arising from self-employment in agriculture	2,045	2,081	1,973
Net farm income	1,880	1,914	1,770

Source: PSE values from Deirdre O'Connor, 'Producer Support for the Irish Dairy Sector in a Changing Policy Environment', Paper presented at 'The Future of Irish Dairying: Oppportunities, Constraints and Policy', University College Dublin, 8 September, 1998; Income figures from CSO, *Output, Input and Income in Agriculture, 1998 Preliminary Estimate*.

the OECD world price for these commodities is set too high in relation to the particular markets served by Irish exports or the quality of product exported. However, the series is the most comprehensive available and is used for the comparisons that follow.[1]

When we compare the value of support received by producers with aggregate income from farming, the results are striking. Over the three years, income from farming on average has been no greater than what has been received in public support from the EU and from Irish consumers and taxpayers. Farmers could save themselves a great deal of trouble if they could persuade policy-makers to simply give them the money instead of requiring them to undertake the business of farming. In fact, the next chapter will show that this option would be much cheaper also from the point of view of the public authorities.

Direct payments and farm income

This conclusion that Irish agricultural income is no greater than the total *support* received by farmers is based on the estimated value of market price support received. It could be argued that the world price gaps used in the calculation of this market price support were too high because they did not allow for the unrealistically low level of existing world prices. It is therefore of interest to look at the contribution of direct payments alone to farm income in more detail. Chapter 2 outlined that direct payments are a feature of drystock (beef and sheep) as well as arable production; milk production is still entirely supported by market price interventions. Thus we need to look at the contribution of direct payments to incomes on drystock and arable farms, bearing in mind that these underestimate the total support provided to these farmers because market prices for beef and cereals are still higher than world prices.

The National Farm Survey conducted by Teagasc, the Irish national agricultural and food development authority, shows the variation in family farm income according to the system of farming. Table 3.2 sets out the results by system for the 1997 survey when the average farm income from farming amounted to £10,800. Drystock farmers have the lowest incomes from farming, with farms involved in cattle rearing earning an average figure barely half of the national farm average. Dairy farmers have the highest income from farming, earning double the national farm average. On the other hand, drystock farmers or their spouse are more likely to have off-farm employment. Particularly striking is the contribution of direct payments on both drystock and arable farms.

TABLE 3.2: National Farm Survey Results by System, 1997.

	All systems	Dairy	Dairy + other	Cattle rearing	Cattle other	Mainly sheep	Mainly tillage
% of farms represented	100	19	14	21	27	14	5
Family farm income (£)	10,798	19,980	17,519	5,594	5,752	7,738	14,676
Direct payments as of FFI	62	22	50	105	98	94	107
Off-farm job holder/spouse (%)	43	30	26	56	42	55	43

Source: Teagasc, National Farm Survey, 1997.

Even on dairy farms, 22 per cent of farm income comes from direct payments even though all dairy support continues to be provided through market intervention because of ancillary beef/arable enterprises on these farms. For those commodities where some substitution of market price support by direct payments has occurred (beef, sheep, arable), direct payments alone are now equal to or even greater than family farm income. This reinforces the conclusion reached on the basis of aggregate statistics above that policy support transfers as a whole now equal the aggregate income of farming.

Another view of the relationship between income from farming and direct payments is shown in Table 3.3. By 1996, only around 5 per cent of farms were *not* in receipt of some form of direct payment. Particular attention can be paid to the proportion of farms where direct payments amounted to or exceeded family farm income. In 1992, this occurred on 16 per cent of farms; by 1996, after the implementation of CAP reform, this proportion increased to 29 per cent. On a further 17 per cent of farms, direct payments made up between 75 and 100 per cent of family farm income. Following the implementation of the Berlin Agenda 2000 in May 1999, it is possible that direct payments will exceed family farm income on more than half of all Irish farmers mid-way through the next decade.

TABLE 3.3: Dependence on direct payments (DPs) for family farm income, per cent of population by dependence category.

Dependence on DPs (%)	1992 (%)	1996 (%)
Negative FFI	5.9	5.2
0	10.7	5.5
0–25	26.9	14.0
25–50	17.9	12.2
50–75	14.5	17.7
75–100	8.5	16.7
100–150	7.3	16.1
>150	8.2	12.6
All	100	100

Source: Keeney, M., 'The distributional effects of direct payments on Irish farm incomes', Teagasc and Trinity College Dublin, mimeo.

Put baldly, the figures suggest that arable and cattle farmers (and sheep farmers are almost in the same situation) would be better off if they ceased farming and were simply given the equivalent value of their current direct payments. Not only would their incomes be higher, but the EU would save on the cost of the remaining market price support and consumers would gain access to cheaper food. It is because the EU gives support on the basis of production that farmers are forced to produce at a loss in order to qualify for support. Of course, no one is suggesting that farmers should cease farming. What we are highlighting here is the way resources are wasted by the system of CAP support and the potential for gain under an alternative farm policy.

4. The cost of subsidising farmers

The Producer Support Estimate discussed in the last chapter measures the value of the support received by farmers from taxpayers and consumers. However, the actual cost borne by taxpayers and consumers in making this transfer is far greater. The difference between what taxpayers and consumers pay in transfers and what farmers actually receive in support is a measure of the cost of making the transfer. No system of transfers is completely costless – administrative costs are always incurred. But the CAP has been a particularly costly mechanism of making transfers because a large proportion of what consumers and taxpayers pay does not end up in farmers' pockets. To keep the two ideas separate, we will refer to *support* when we are talking about the value of transfers from the perspective of farmers and use *transfers* to refer to the burden placed on taxpayers and consumers of providing this support. The relationship between the value of support received and the cost of transfers made is a measure of the transfer efficiency of agricultural policy.

There are two main reasons why the CAP is a costly mechanism of making transfers. Firstly, the CAP's market price support policy is costly to operate and secondly, there are significant leakages of support away from the intended beneficiaries. The main reason for the high operational cost is the reliance on intervention. This is particularly clear in the case of beef which is a high-value fresh product but whose value drops dramatically once it is put into intervention storage and frozen. In addition, intervention storage itself is costly in terms of the physical and financial costs it incurs.

Perhaps more serious is the way in which part of the transfers paid by consumers and taxpayers benefit groups other than EU farmers. We referred to one problem in Chapter 2, namely, that the CAP price support mechanisms provide support to farm commodities at the processing level and rely on competition to ensure that this support is passed back to farmers. Inevitably, part of the support is captured by processors in the form of higher margins.

Another example is the way in which benefits intended for farmers leak out to input suppliers and landowners. A comparison of the cost of the same chemical in New Zealand (where farmers compete at world prices) and in Europe (where farmers are protected by the CAP) showed that the manufacturer was able to charge a much higher price in Europe. Or take the case of the milk-quota regime intended to benefit dairy farmers.[2] Many smaller dairy farmers decide not to remain in milk production and sell or lease their quota to other dairy farmers who wish to expand. The value of the milk support is then capitalised into the value of the quota. In turn, this is captured by the farmer *leaving* the industry and not by the farmer who remains in milk production. Instead, his or her costs of production are increased by the overhead cost of acquiring the quota. And if a farmer needs to rent land in order to expand, the higher profitability of farming due to price support is simply reflected in higher rents, thus benefiting the landowner rather than the working farmer.

But the biggest problem is that some of the transfers mainly benefit those countries which import the EU's export surpluses. Export subsidies lower the price to importing countries as much as they raise the price to EU farmers. The Russian consumer getting

TABLE 4.1: Structure of the Irish farm transfers account.

Total transfers made	Total transfers received
1. Transfer from EU taxpayers	7. Total transfer
2. Transfer from EU consumers	8. Support received by Irish farmers
3. Total EU transfer	9. Operational costs
4. Transfer from Irish taxpayers	10. Leakages to Irish non-farm roups
5. Transfer from Irish consumers	11. Leakages to third countries
6. Total domestic transfer	12. Total transfer

Notes: Transfer efficiency is defined as the ratio of item 8 to item 12. Item 1, Transfer from EU taxpayers, is also referred to as the *EU budget transfer*. Item 2, Transfer from EU consumers, is also referred to as the *EU trade transfer*.

EU butter and beef at knock-down prices is as grateful to the CAP as the Irish farmer is. This follows directly from the fact noted in the previous chapter that existing world prices are depressed by the practice of supporting agriculture in most industrialised countries.

To clarify the different concepts used in this chapter, it is helpful to examine what we will call the Irish farm transfers account. The entries in this account are set out in Table 4.1. The left-hand side shows the sources of transfers. They include both EU consumers and taxpayers as well as Irish consumers and taxpayers. The right-hand side represents the beneficiaries of these transfers. In an ideal world, the support received by Irish farmers would equal the sum of the left-hand transfers. But because of the operational costs and leakages discussed above, only a proportion of these transfers actually benefits farmers. This proportion is what we define as the transfer efficiency of the CAP. What we want to do in the rest of this chapter is to fill in the numbers associated with each of the entries in this table in order to calculate the actual efficiency of CAP transfers.

Of particular interest is the cost of the transfer borne by EU consumers and taxpayers. The external transfer from the EU is often referred to as the *national* gain from the operation of the CAP. This is because it purports to represent a net addition to national income and is not simply a transfer from one group in Irish society to another. In fact, this interpretation exaggerates the national gain from the CAP as we shall see.in Chapter 7.

The national gain due to the CAP

Producer support is made up of market price support and budgetary payments. Budget expenditure on agricultural policy is financed primarily from the EU budget. Irish taxpayers contribute partly through paying their share of EU expenditure but also because of the co-financing required for certain EU schemes. For instance, market price support is paid for ultimately by consumers. For products sold on the domestic market, it is the domestic consumer who pays; for products sold elsewhere in the EU, it is the EU consumer who pays. Adding together the budget transfers (paid by the EU taxpayer) and the market price support paid by the EU consumer (on Irish agricultural exports to the rest of the EU) gives the external transfer arising from the operation of the Common Agricultural Policy. Estimates of the size of this transfer made by the Department of Agriculture and Food are reproduced in Table 4.2 below.

The gross budget receipts represent the total transfer of resources to Ireland through FEOGA, calculated by adding Guarantee expenditure to Guidance receipts. However, Irish taxpayers contribute to the cost of running the CAP. Hence, the net national gain from CAP budget transfers is measured by the Net Budget Effect (NBE) which deducts Ireland's estimated contribution to the FEOGA budget. The 'trade effect' is measured by estimating the price gap which exists between Irish and world prices for each commodity and applying this gap to the value of Irish

TABLE 4.2: Combined budget and trade effect (£m).

	1995 (£m)	1996 (£m)	1997 (£m)
Gross budget receipts	1,383.5	1,638.0	1,528.1
Less Irish contribution to FEOGA	−286.7	−295.3	−268.5
Net budget effect	1,096.7	1,342.8	1,259.6
Trade effect	758.0	536.9	467.7
Gross budget and trade effect	2,141.5	2,174.9	1,995.8
Net budget and trade effect	1,854.8	1,879.7	1,727.3
Memo item:			
Producer Support Estimate (PSE)	2,037	1,917	1,690

Source: Department of Agriculture and Food, *Annual Review and Outlook 1998*; Producer Support Estimate is from.Table 3.1.

exports and imports to and from the EU. Between 1995 and 1997 these combined effects amounted to £1.7–£1.9 billion. What is interesting is that these EU transfers alone are of a similar size to the Producer Support Estimate presented in Chapter 3. This is despite the fact that the world price gaps used by the Department of Agriculture and Food to calculate the trade effect are smaller those used in the PSE calculation in the previous chapter.

A transfer of £1.7 billion amounted to 4 per cent of GNP in 1997, which is a significant contribution to the economy. Given the political attention to the size of Ireland's receipts from the Structural Funds, it is of interest to compare the size of the budget and trade transfers received as a result of the CAP with transfers from the EU's Structural Funds and other receipts (Table 4.3). For this purpose, it is appropriate to compare the CAP gross budget and trade effects with Structural Fund receipts because the Irish taxpayer contribution is proportionally the same in both cases. Even in 1997, the CAP transfers were worth double the transfers from all other EU sources. FEOGA Guidance transfers are double-counted in this comparison as they are both a CAP receipt and a part of the Structural Funds, but excluding them from CAP receipts does not alter the conclusion materially.

However, this comparison is not strictly comparing like with like. Non-CAP receipts add directly to national income. The CAP receipts, as indicated above, measure the cost to the EU of

TABLE 4.3: CAP transfers compared to other EU receipts.

	1995 (£m)	1996 (£m)	1997 (£m)
FEOGA Guidance	142.9	150.6	165.9
Social Fund	256.2	252.9	271.0
Regional Fund	358.1	297.1	356.2
Cohesion Fund	102.0	137.1	162.7
Fishery Fund	4.6	6.5	10.1
Miscellaneous	9.2	10.8	20.9
Total EU receipts	873.0	855.0	986.8
CAP gross budget and trade effect	2,141.5	2,174.9	1,995.8

Source: Department of Finance; CAP gross budget and trade effect from Table 4.2.

making the transfer but not necessarily the value of the transfer received by the Irish economy. For example, the CAP transfers include the cost of export subsidies. Much of the benefit of these subsidies accrues to consumers in importing countries rather than Irish producers.[3] Other CAP transfers are payments for services provided (e.g. storage) so that their net contribution to national income is less than their nominal value. Nonetheless, the reason for the fierce Irish defence of the CAP is revealed by these figures. As far as Ireland is concerned, the CAP is perceived to have been a much more powerful instrument of EU regional policy than the EU's Regional Fund has been. Whether this is, in fact, the case is examined later in Chapter 7.

Domestic transfers to agriculture

The previous section outlined estimates of EU transfers to Irish agriculture. Because of its strong export orientation, the external EU transfer is often assumed to be the predominant element of the total transfer to Irish agriculture. However, the internal transfer from Irish taxpayers and consumers is significant and is growing in importance. This internal transfer is made up of five elements:

1. the national cost of co-financing EU Guarantee Section schemes;
2. the national cost of co-financing EU socio-structural aids;
3. the national cost of purely national aid schemes to agriculture;
4. the Irish taxpayer contribution to the cost of the EU FEOGA budget and
5. the cost to consumers of higher food prices due to the CAP.

The first three of these items are included in the budget of the Department of Agriculture and Food. Total expenditure of this Department was £769m in 1997, of which £353m was recouped from the EU, leaving net expenditure of £416m. The cost of the three support components was around £190m. The balance of the net expenditure represents administrative and regulatory expenditure (for example, veterinary and plant health regulation) and research and education expenditure which would continue in a no-support environment.

To this sum must be added the cost to Irish taxpayers of the overall operation of the CAP. Each year the Irish exchequer transfers its share of the overall EU budget to Brussels. As the CAP accounts for around 50 per cent of total EU spending, then that share of the Irish contribution represents what Irish taxpayers provide indirectly to the support of Irish agriculture. This contribution was netted out in calculating the external EU transfer in the previous section, but must be included here as part of the internal transfer.

Finally, the consumer cost of higher market prices must be added. This is calculated by taking the world price gap and applying to it that part of Irish agricultural production which is sold on the domestic market. Using the O'Connor price gap estimates, the cost to Irish consumers amounted to £487m in 1997 and considerably more in earlier years. This is equivalent to a consumer tax on food of this magnitude to support farm incomes.

What does this mean to individual families? In 1997, the transfer from each household amounted to £753 per year. Household Budget Survey data for that year show an average household expenditure on food of £3,692. Therefore, the consumer food tax amounts to 20 per cent of the food expenditure of the average household. As a percentage of household disposable income, the transfer amounts to an average of 5 per cent per household. Food is currently zero-rated for VAT purposes in Ireland. One can imagine the political outcry if someone suggested taxing food at the higher rate of VAT! Yet this is the effect of present CAP policies and it passes virtually without comment.

Table 4.4 shows that the cost to Irish taxpayers and consumers of supporting farm income now amounts to over £900 million annually, or half of the value of income from farming. As the Irish GNP growth rate exceeds the EU average, our share of the total FEOGA budget will increase over time, and thus so will the cost to Irish taxpayers of the present CAP. Already, there was a sharp increase in these costs in 1998 to £393m. The more

TABLE 4.4: Irish taxpayer and consumer transfer to
Irish agriculture (£m).

	1995 (£m)	1996 (£m)	1997 (£m)
National cost of financing CAP market regimes[1]	51.2	113.2	69.4
National cost of financing EU socio-structural aids[2]	60.4	81.3	60.3
Cost of national aid schemes to agriculture[3]	50.5	48.8	40.0
Irish contribution to FEOGA budget	286.7	295.3	268.5
Consumer cost of higher food prices	790.1	621.4	481.5
Total transfer from Irish taxpayers and consumers to farmers	1,238.9	1,160.0	935.0

1 These include CAP financing, REPS and early retirement.
2 These include on-farm investment, headage payments, farm diversification'
  etc.
3 These include disease control, damage relief, livestock improvement, etc.
Source: Deirdre O'Connor, op. cit.

the £1.7 billion in support to Irish farmers is financed by an
internal transfer from Irish taxpayers and consumers, the more
urgent it becomes to examine the justification and rationale of
this expenditure. The principal justification in the past has been
that farmers suffer from lower incomes on average than the
rest of society. In the following chapter the continued validity of
this claim is subjected to critical scrutiny.

The transfer efficiency of farm support

We conclude this chapter by bringing together the various elements making up the total transfers to Irish agriculture from
both EU and Irish sources. This is done by specifying the
amounts in the Irish farm transfers equation for a particular
year. We choose 1997 because the world price gaps used by
O'Connor in calculating the value of support to farmers are
closer to those used by the Department of Agriculture and Food
in calculating the value of the trade transfer in that year.

We stress again that the total transfers are not the same as
the total support received by farmers documented in Table 3.1.
This is because some of the transfers are deflected into the costs
of making the transfer, while other transfers leak away to other

TABLE 4.5: The Irish transfers account in 1997.

Total transfers made	£m	Total transfers received	£m
1. Net transfer from EU taxpayers	1,260	8. Support received by Irish farmers	1,680
2. Transfer from EU consumers	468	9. Operational costs and leakages	957
3. Total EU transfer	1,727		
4. Transfer from Irish taxpayers	438		
5. Transfer from Irish consumers	482		
6. Total domestic transfer	920		
7. Total transfer	2,647	12. Total transfer	2,647

beneficiaries and never actually reach farmers. The composition of these transfers is shown in Table 4.5. The EU contribution is about two-thirds of the total transfers and the domestic contribution about one-third. Comparing the size of transfers to the value of support received by farmers is a measure of the transfer cost. In the case of Irish agriculture, more than one-third of transfers (36 per cent) do not reach their intended beneficiaries. This underlines the inefficiencies of the present system and suggests strongly the potential for economic gain from a change.[4]

5. Are average farm incomes low?

Much of the justification for the massive transfer to farmers documented in the previous chapter is that farm incomes lag behind the incomes of the non-agricultural sector and that farmers are a relatively disadvantaged group in Irish society. Indeed, the average income from farming activity per farm in 1997 amounted to only £10,798, which compares unfavourably to the average industrial wage of around £15,000 in that year. However, the calculation of average farm incomes and their comparison with non-farm incomes is a conceptual and statistical minefield. This chapter provides a short guide to the pitfalls. It will show that the average living standards of farm families are now at least as high as the rest of society and it will also discuss some explanations for the relative improvement in farm incomes.

In moving from aggregate farm income to average farm income it is first necessary to divide the total by the number of farmers. While this appears a straightforward step, what is meant by the number of farmers is an elastic concept and the appropriate divisor is far from clear. Second, the nature of the income comparison with non-farm groups must be defined. Employee earnings are a return to their labour alone, while farm income represents the return not only to a farmer's labour and management input, but also the return on his or her own capital used in farm production. Those interested in the efficiency of resource-use would want to separately identify the returns to individual factors of production. In comparing overall income levels between groups, however, differences in the sources of income are irrelevant.

On the other hand, the fact that farmers own land which may appreciate in value over time may not be irrelevant in making welfare comparisons. Hence, a third issue in income comparisons is how to make allowances for differences in wealth and capital gains. A fourth issue is that only taking account of income from farming provides a very misleading indicator of the income of farm households. Farm households now obtain the majority of their income from non-farm sources, either from off-farm employment or government transfers. Income comparisons based on the total income of farm households are a more reliable indicator of the income status of farmers than relying on income from farming alone. A final issue is that farming is not a homogeneous industry. It contains a wide range of farm sizes and types, and a high average income is no guarantee that there are not farm households with incomes low enough to classify them as poor. Distributional issues of this kind are discussed in Chapter 6.

Numbers engaged in farming

Table 5.1 gives a number of estimates of those engaged in farming from a variety of sources. If we assume that farmers are those who own a farm, then the number of farms (and thus farmers)

TABLE 5.1: Estimates of the numbers engaged in farming.

	1998
Number of farms	146,300
Employment in agriculture (ILO definition)	129,800
Total number working on farms, full and part time	275,100
Full time job equivalent of work done on farms (AWUs)	200,200

Source: Department of Agriculture and Food, *Annual Review and Outlook 1998*.

can be obtained from the regular CSO Farm Structure Surveys. There were 146,000 farms in 1998, compared to 162,000 in 1992 and an estimated 217,000 in 1987. Part of the decline in numbers represents the consolidation and amalgamation of farms during this period but there was also a significant definitional change in 1991 which excluded farms under 2ha from the farm population, as compared to 1ha previously. The number of farms clearly depends on where this threshold is drawn. Even the current threshold is low when it comes to defining a farmer. It hardly makes sense to consider a person with just 5ha of land a farmer, unless he or she is engaged in intensive horticulture. But the CSO statistics on the number of farm holders count everyone with more than 2ha. They also include as farmers elderly people who may still own land but are not running the farm as a commercial business. For both reasons, these statistics tend to exaggerate the actual number of farmers. In 1996, when choosing the sample for its National Farm Survey, Teagasc omitted farms below 2 economic size units (an economic size unit is an EU measure of the size of the farm business). This deleted 14 per cent of the farm population but only 2 per cent of the farm output. This underlines the fact that the number of farm holders exaggerates the number of practising farmers.

Another approach is to base the number of farmers on the number who define their principal occupation as farming. This is the approach taken in the annual Labour Force Surveys and 129,800 people replied that their principal occupation was farming in 1998. This number includes farm workers (including assisting relatives) as well as farmers. However, this statistic is unsatisfactory because there are many other people (not least the spouses of farmers) who contribute some labour to agricultural activity. A third source, the annual CSO Agricultural Labour Input survey attempts to count all those who contribute some labour to agriculture. In 1998, over a quarter of a million people made some contribution to farming. By taking account of the number of hours worked by each of these persons this number can be transformed into a full-time equivalent number, in 1998 just over 200,000.

Average Income from Farming

Based on the above distinctions between the numbers engaged in farming, there are four different approaches to estimating average income from farming:

1. one approach is to divide aggregate farm income (income arising in agriculture taken from the CSO Economic Accounts for Agriculture, see Chapter 1) by employment in agriculture to calculate the average income from farming per agricultural worker. If the residual labour income (non-agricultural income) is divided by the remaining employment (non-agricultural employment), a parallel measure of average non-agricultural income can be estimated. Taking the ratio of average agricultural income to average non-agricultural income yields a *disparity index* (the oldest method of comparing farm and non-farm incomes).[5] The calculation is simple to make given a set of national accounts, and because each country has the relevant data it is easy to use the index to make cross-country comparisons. However, it is a misleading guide to relative average farm incomes given its assumption that those in farming only receive income from farming, the fact that it ignores interest costs and that it includes farm workers in the total of agricultural employment.

2. a second approach is to divide aggregate farm income by the number of farm holdings (taken from the CSO Agricultural Farm Structures Survey) to show average income per farm.

The trouble with this indicator is the very wide definition of what is a farm. Included in the denominator are very small holdings as well as holdings of whatever size which are worked by farmers beyond retirement age.

3. a third approach is to divide aggregate farm income by total annual work units (AWUs) (taken from the CSO Agricultural Labour Input Survey) to show average income per full-time job equivalent. This is a good measure to use if one is interested in estimating the return to labour in the agricultural sector. As a measure of overall income, it has the drawback that it does not provide information on the labour input of the typical farm household, so it is not possible to estimate the total income from farming of farm households from these data.

4. a fourth approach is to use Teagasc's National Farm Survey (NFS) data to get an estimate of average family farm income. In particular, by confining attention to full-time farms (in the NFS these are defined as farms whose agricultural activity is sufficient to provide employment for at least 0.7 of a labour unit) it is possible to reduce some of the heterogeneity which would be present if all farms are included.

Figure 5.1 shows Department of Agriculture and Food estimates of income from agriculture from 1991 to 1997 using three of these definitions in comparison to the average industrial wage. There are considerable variations between the results. In 1997, for example, the average income per farm was £13,213, the average income per Annual Work Unit was £9,489 (both from CSO data) and the average income per farm according to Teagasc was £10,798 (this Teagasc estimate is for all farms and not just full-time farms). All three measures of average farm income show an upward trend from 1991 to 1996. For 1997, the National Farm Survey indicates a fall of 1 per cent in family farm income, average income per farm declined by 5 per cent, while average income per AWU rose by 2 per cent. For all three measures, average income from farming activities is below the average industrial wage.

FIG 5.1: Average income (IR£) from farming, 1991–97.

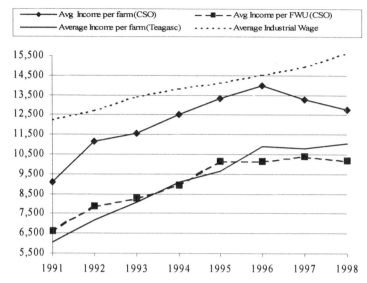

Source: Department of Agriculture and Food, *Annual Review and Outlook 1998*.

FIG 5.2: Alternative asset returns compared to inflation.

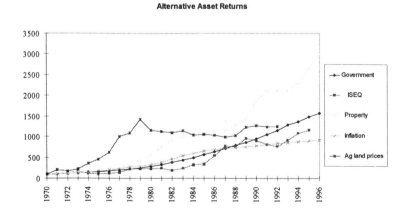

Taking account of land ownership

The average farm income indicators discussed so far ignore the fact that farm families often hold large quantities of wealth, particularly in the form of land. If two families have the same current income but one family derives much of this income from the ownership of a significant capital asset such as land, most people would feel that the second family was in some sense better off. Land ownership is a form of additional security in that it can be sold and turned into potential spending power on consumer goods and services. Land, like other capital assets, can also give rise to capital gains (and losses) which arguably should be taken into account in measuring the economic status of farmers.

Of course, it is real (and not only nominal) gains which make a positive contribution to income. Figure 5.2 shows how agricultural land prices have changed since 1970 in comparison to other property assets and the rate of inflation. The sharp increase in land prices up to 1979 stands out, as does their gentle fall until about 1988 when prices began to recover. Although the increase in agricultural land prices does not compare to increases in urban property values, they have nonetheless stayed comfortably ahead of inflation. The real value of farm assets has increased over time.

However, it is not easy to combine current income and wealth into an acceptable single indicator of economic status. Farmers protest that they do not view their land as wealth in the sense that it could be converted into cash. Indeed, turnover of land is extraordinarily low. Having averaged around 21,000 hectares during 1991/96, only 11,134 hectares of farmland were sold in 1997, or approximately 0.2 per cent of the total agricultural and forest land area. Agricultural land in Ireland is not a very liquid asset. Capital gains also differ from current income in terms of their uncertainty and liquidity. For these reasons, agricultural income measures do not normally take these wealth effects into account, but it is important to keep them in mind when making inter-group income comparisons.

TABLE 5.2: Farmholders with off-farm jobs versus farmers with no off-farm jobs, 1997.

	All systems	Dairy	Dairy + other	Cattle rearing	Cattle other	Mainly sheep	Mainly tillage
Family farmincome (£)							
No job	13,016	20,933	18,290	6,558	6,719	9,775	15,546
Job	5,413	12,369	10,273	4,561	3,712	4,771	11,476

Source: Department of Agriculture and Food, *Annual Review and Outlook, 1998*.

Farm household income

People working on farms increasingly have off-farm income. The biggest criticism of the previous indicators of average farm income is that farm income alone gives a misleading picture of the economic status of farm families. Since 1993, Teagasc has published data in its National Farm Surveys which indicate the number of farmers and/or spouses who participate in off-farm employment. In 1997 farmers and/or spouses had an off-farm source of employment on 43 per cent of farms, a significant increase over the 1993 figure of 31 per cent. There is also a clear inverse relationship between income from farming and off-farm income (Table 5.2). If part of the reason why income from farming is low is because the farmer has an off-farm job, it makes sense to aggregate these incomes and to look at total farm household income when assessing its overall adequacy.

In discussing the measurement of farm income EUROSTAT, the European Union Statistical Office, makes the point in the following way:

> An income measure which aims to be a proxy for the standard of living of the agricultural community, though clearly not an exact one, will need to cover income from all sources, not just that from farming activity. It will focus on the household or family unit rather than the farmer (agricultural holder) alone. And because not all the income is available to be spent, due allowance has to be made for taxation, social contributions and other transfers. The name given to the residual income is (Net) Disposable Income, and this forms a widely

accepted concept for assessing the income situation of farm households.[6]

To examine farm household income again raises the definitional question of what we consider to be a farm household. We can choose between defining a farm household as one where (1) income from farming is the main source of the total income of the entire household; (2) income from farming is the main source of income of the head of household; (3) the principal occupation of the head of household is farming, irrespective of income; or (4) the broadest definition, as a household which is associated with a farm holding and thus which has some income from farming. EUROSTAT uses the second definition in cross-national comparisons, while Irish analysis using the Household Budget Survey uses the fourth definition.

Household budget survey comparisons

The changing importance of the different income sources of farm households emerges clearly from Table 5.3. Income from farming now contributes only half of their total income (defining farm households as those households which have some income from farming). Other direct income, mainly wage employment, has grown steadily while income from social welfare transfer payments has fluctuated in importance depending on the state of the farm-income cycle when the survey was conducted.

Table 5.4 compares the average incomes of farm households with those of urban households, other rural households, and the

TABLE 5.3: Percentage of total farm household income from all sources, 1973–94

	1973 (%)	1980 (%)	1987 (%)	1994(%)
Farming	70.1	58.3	54.2	53.0
Other direct income	19.1	26.3	17.6	35.0
Transfer payments	10.8	15.2	28.3	12.0
Gross income	100.0	100.0	100.0	100.0

Source: Household Budget Surveys.

TABLE 5.4: Averate annual household income 1994–95

	Farm house-holds(£)	Other rural households(£)	Urban house-holds(£)	State average(£)
Farming income	9,938	313	34	1,036
Non farm employment	5,746	10,375	14,031	12,249
Other direct income	729	1,087	1,899	1,566
Total state transfers	2,169	3,281	2,987	2,992
Gross income	18,582	15,055	18,951	17,842
less total direct taxation	1,938	2,356	3,729	3,183
Disposable income	16,644	12,699	15,222	14,659
Persons per household	3.63	3.31	3.22	3.28
Gross income per householder	5,116	4,551	5,894	5,441
Disposable Income per householder	4,583	3,839	4,735	4,471

Source: Household Budget Survey Preliminary Results 1994/95, CSO.

national average. It indicates that farm households, on average, had a slightly lower gross income (£18,582) than urban households, but a higher disposable income (£16,644) due to lower taxes. However, when the larger size of farm households is taken into account, both gross and disposable income per farm household member were lower than for urban householders. Income for farm households was, in all cases, higher than for rural non-farm households.

Further light on the relative size of farm incomes comes from a survey of farm households based on the second definition above (i.e. based on the income from farming of the head of household) conducted for EUROSTAT on the basis of the 1987 Household Budget Survey. EUROSTAT calls this a 'narrow' definition of farm households and refers to the definition used in the Irish Household Budget Survey, which includes all households with some income from farming as farm households, as the 'broad' definition. Table 5.5 shows that the average disposable income per unit (household, household member or consumer unit[7]) of farm households defined in the 'narrow' way was substantially above the equivalent figures resulting from the use of the 'broad' definition. This was because the households that derived some income from farming, but where it was

TABLE 5.5: Numbers of households and average disposable income per unit for alternative definitions of an agricultural household, 1987.

Classification criterion	Households (000s)	Income per households (£)	Income per household member(£)	Income per consumer (£)
'Narrow' definition (head of household, main income)	84.5	12,867	3,266	4,529
'Broad' definition (household with any income from farming)	206.7	10,600	2,837	3,910
'Marginal' households ('broad' minus 'narrow')	122.2	9,032	2,512	3,447
All households in Ireland		10,101	2,882	3,854

Source: Eurostat, Total Income of Agricultural Households, 1996.

not the main income of the head of household, had disposable incomes that were well below those of the 'narrow' group (some 30 per cent less).

In Ireland, households which are headed by a person who regards him or herself as a farmer fall into two groups of similar numerical size. One consists of operators mainly dependent on farming for their livelihoods (corresponding to the 'narrow' definition). The other is made up of people who call themselves farmers but who are mainly dependent on social welfare benefits and who have substantially lower average levels of disposable income. When the incomes of farm households are compared with the national all-household average, the influence of the classification of farm households becomes clear. Applying the 'narrow' definition results in average incomes per unit that were about one-quarter to one-fifth higher than the all-household figure. Even with the 'broad' definition, however, the average income level per household was around the national average in 1987. While income per household member was below the national average, when the differing composition of households was taken into account, the income per consumer unit in farm households exceeded the 1987 national average.

Farmer taxation

One of the factors contributing to the higher disposable income of farm households is the low level of direct taxation which they pay in relation to their gross income. The taxation of farmers has been a controversial topic ever since the dramatic rise in farm incomes in the 1970s (see Figure 2.1). The state experimented with a special regime for the taxation of agricultural profits in the 1980s. This was abolished in 1987 and income from farming is now assessed for tax on the same basis as income from any other trading activity. A special simplified taxation return is used by most farmers to determine whether a liability to tax is likely to arise or not. In the tax year 1998/99 an estimated 92,000 farmers were assessed for tax on their profits. In addition there are about 18,200 farmers who are not assessed annually but whose position is reviewed periodically – thus, the total number of farmers on record with the Revenue Commissioners stands at approximately 110,000 which is close to the total number of farms identified above.

The yield from farmers in respect of income tax on farming profits was estimated to be approximately £75m in 1998. Given the £1 billion in direct payments which farmers received in that year, it seems an extraordinarily low figure. Farmers also pay income tax through the PAYE system on income earned from off-farm employment. This is estimated at £92m for 1995/96 (the latest year for which data is available) and was paid by some 25,324 individuals or couples. In addition, farmers contribute PRSI and levy payments through the self-assessment system. Their contributions in 1997 are estimated at £26.0m. Farmers contributed 1.6 per cent of the total income tax take in 1996 (the last year for which data is available). Table 5.6 summarises the position from 1992–98. Table 5.7 compares the average tax paid per farmer with the average paid by a PAYE worker and a self-employed person. On average, farmers pay less than a quarter of the tax paid by other taxpayers. One of the reasons for this is the broad definition of who is a farmer.

TABLE 5.6: Farmer income tax and PRSI, 1992–98 (£m).

Year	Income tax		PRSI	Total
	Farm Profits	PAYE		
1992	48	43	12.3	103.3
1993	56†	56	23.0	135
1994	90†	71	28.1	189.1
1995	70	78	29.9	177.9
1996	78	92	25.2	195.2
1997	85	N/A	26.0	N/A
1998‡	75	N/A	N/A	N/A

Note: † *Includes amounts collected under the 1993 tax amnesty – £1m in 1993 and £23.5m in 1994.*
 ‡ *Estimate only.*
Source: Department of Agriculture and Food, *Annual Review and Outlook 1997* based on Revenue Commissioners data.

TABLE 5.7: Average income tax paid by sector, 1991–97.

Year	PAYE	Farmers	Other self-employed
	£	£	£
1991	3,541	601	2,562
1992	3,633	710	3,154
1993‡	3,849	782	3,586
1994‡	3,894	892	3,798
1995	4,049	932	3,707
1996 †	4,308	1,021	4,049
1997 †	4,649	1,097	4,748

Note: † *Provisional;* ‡ *Excludes amnesty yields in 1993 and 1994 under the 1993 tax amnesty.*
Source: Department of Agriculture and Food, *Annual Review and Outlook 1997* based on Revenue Commissioners data.

For the same reason that a broad definition reduces the perceived average farm income, it also reduces the perceived average tax paid. However, even allowing for this, the low average tax paid per farmer remains puzzling.

Factors behind the relative farm income improvement

Using farm household disposable income as the appropriate indicator as recommended by EUROSTAT, this chapter shows that average farm incomes now exceed the level of incomes of non-farm households and that there is no longer a generalised income problem in farming. Chapter 3 emphasised the huge importance of public support to agriculture relative to farm incomes. It would not be surprising to assume that this massive support has been the main reason for the improvement in farm incomes relative to non-farm incomes. However, it is important to look behind the figures to understand why farm incomes were low in the past. Relative farm incomes would have risen anyway, regardless of the level of support.

Farm incomes were low in the past because of the extensive underemployment on farms, because farmers generally had a low level of education and because farmers on average were elderly. The biggest single factor in the relative improvement in average farm incomes has been the availability of off-farm employment, not least in rural areas. This has helped to alleviate the problem of underemployment by facilitating part-time farming. By providing an alternative income source it has put a floor under farm incomes. If there are no jobs available, agriculture acts as a labour reserve, absorbing people who have no alternative employment opportunities. The economic diversification of rural areas and improved transport possibilities have provided alternative possibilities. Farmers are no longer locked into agriculture at very low incomes.

Linked to this is the relative improvement of education levels among farmers compared to the non-farm population. It is not so long ago that the son chosen to take over the farm was taken out of school at the earliest possible opportunity. As a result, education levels among farmers were low compared to the general population. A wide range of studies has demonstrated the link between higher education levels and higher earnings. As the education of younger farmers improves, the average educational level among farmers is rising, and with it average farm income.

Finally, low average farm incomes are partly explained by the high average age of farmers and the large number, almost one-fifth, who are beyond retirement age. While this age distribution is changing only slowly, the income situation of elderly farmers has been greatly improved by the extension to them of the social welfare contributory pension scheme and by the general improvement in the level of social transfers. Given the weight of this group in the farm population, their improved incomes have also helped to raise the level of the average farm income over time.

What this means is that the main effect of the massive support to farmers documented in the previous chapter has been to encourage more people to remain in farming, rather than raising their average income. In the absence of agricultural support, there would undoubtedly be fewer people in the industry, but there is no reason why those who would remain would want to work for less than the average farm income today, given the wider availability of off-farm income possibilities. The question raised by this analysis is whether keeping more people in farming yields benefits commensurate with the £900 million which the Irish public alone contributes for this purpose.

6. The distribution of farm income and support

Because of the heterogeneous nature of the agricultural sector, covering as it does a wide range of farm sizes and farming types, the average farm income figure is rather meaningless. The average combines a relatively small number of large farm businesses, yielding a high income, with a much larger number of medium and small farm business yielding a much lower income. An approach that will allow more focus on distributional questions is to examine the proportion of farm households which have an income below a certain threshold. Either National Farm Survey (NFS), Household Budget Survey (HBS) or, more recently, the ESRI's Living in Ireland (LII) Survey data can be used for this purpose.[8]

The NFS only provides information on the distribution of income from farming. Because it ignores off-farm income, it cannot be used to say anything about the welfare of farm households. On the other hand, its income data can be cross-tabulated in many different ways to throw light on how incomes differ by farm size, by farming system, by farm region, by farm household demography, etc. The HBS and LII data allow the total income of farm households to be compared to household incomes of other social groups and inferences can be drawn from these data about the extent of poverty among farm households and how this compares to other households in the state. On the other hand, the published data do not allow any disaggregation of farm households to examine the distribution of total household income by different types of farms or farm households.

This chapter first makes use of NFS data to highlight some characteristics of the distribution of income from farming. Of particular interest here is the contribution which agricultural support policy makes to the distribution of income from farming. Some tentative estimates of how agricultural support is distributed suggest that larger farmers gain most from market price support. The recent shift in CAP income support instruments from market price support to direct payments for a number of commodities raises the question of whether direct payments are more equally distributed among farmers than the market price support they replaced. Although this question cannot be answered directly, some evidence on how the £1 billion of direct payments influences the distribution of income from farming is reviewed. We identify which schemes have the most progressive impact on the distribution of farming income and which schemes largely benefit higher income farmers.

The chapter then considers the evidence on the extent of farm poverty. For this purpose it is appropriate to focus on the total income of farm households rather than income from farming alone. In recent years, there has been a sharp drop in the proportion of farm households with incomes below the poverty line and an even sharper drop in the proportion of all poor households which are farm households. Farm households now make up less than 5 per cent of all households in the state

TABLE 6.1: Distribution of family farm income before and after CAP reform.

Farm-income deciles	1992 (Percent of total income)	1996 (Percent of total income)
Bottom	-1.92	-0.98
2	0.90	1.72
3	2.14	3.02
4	3.22	4.28
5	4.63	5.58
6	6.57	7.27
7	9.07	9.71
8	12.55	13.23
9	18.76	18.56
Top 10%	44.08	37.61
Top 5%	29.51	24.12
Total	100	100

Source: Keeney, M., unpublished tabulations based on the National Farm Survey, Trinity College, Dublin, mimeo.

classified as poor. The recently announced Farm Assist Scheme is likely to make a bigger contribution to improving their welfare than any modification of agricultural policy measures.

Who benefits from agricultural support?

Income from farming is unequally distributed. In 1992, when all support was provided through market intervention, 63 per cent of farm income accrued to the top 20 per cent of farms. Conversely, the 60 per cent of farms with the lowest farm incomes shared 25 per cent of aggregate income from farming. This inequality was less pronounced in 1996 after the implementation of the CAP reform, although it was still substantial. The top 20 per cent of farms shared 56 per cent of farm income, while the share of the bottom 60 per cent of farms had increased to 31 per cent (Table 6.1).

CAP reform contributed to this more equal distribution of farm income after 1992. Direct payments are distributed more equally across farms, and the greater reliance on direct payments in total income from farming has resulted in less inequality in the distribution of this income. At the same time, CAP reform also resulted in the distribution of direct payments themselves becoming much more skewed, and further moves to increase the role of direct payments may not have the same inequality-reducing effect. This apparent paradox can be explained as follows.

Before CAP reform in 1992, direct payments were targeted on farms in less favoured areas, as well as sheep and suckler cow producers, farm groups with predominantly below-average incomes. The close correspondence between the shares of total direct payments paid and the proportion of farms in each income group in 1992 suggests that, on average, pre-1992 direct payments were spread fairly evenly throughout the farm population (Table 6.1). The growing importance of premia payments since 1992, paid to compensate for reductions in market support prices to beef and arable farmers, has led to a more skewed distribution of direct payments in recent years. This is because payments made across-the-board to compensate farmers for a reduction in market price support inevitably benefit farms with the greatest volume of production (as did the market price support for which it substitutes), unless specific modulation is built in. Only very limited modulation was built in to the new direct payment schemes introduced by CAP reform – none at all in the case of arable aid. The ceilings on the number of animals eligible for support under the two special beef premium schemes at ninety animals each were set very high in Irish conditions, as were the ceilings on the numbers of ewe premia. Thus it is not surprising that the share of direct payments received by the 20 per cent of farms with the highest farm income increased from 30 per cent in 1992 to 37 per cent in 1997 (Table 6.2).

Nonetheless, these figures do not suggest the extreme maldistribution of support typically expressed along the lines that 'the top 20 per cent of farmers get 80 per cent of payments'. This is only partly because the variation in farm size within Ireland is much less than it is across Europe. The main reason is that the really top-earners among Irish farmers, the dairy producers, receive relatively little of their support in the form of direct payments. If dairy farmers are compensated for reductions in milk

TABLE 6.2: Percent of total direct payments
to each farm-income decile.

	1992	1994	1997
	Percent of total direct payments (%)		
Decile 1	5.3	3.6	5
Decile 2	4.2	3.4	4
Decile 3	6.4	5.1	5
Decile 4	7.0	5.7	6
Decile 5	8.9	7.2	7
Decile 6	10.6	11.4	9
Decile 7	13.0	12.2	12
Decile 8	14.9	12.5	15
Decile 9	16.0	16.7	15
Decile 10	13.9	22.2	22
All	100	100	100

Source: Mary Keeney, Alan Matthews and Jim Frawley, 'The distribution of direct payments in Irish agriculture', Paper read to the Dublin Economics Workshop conference, Kenmare, 1997; Department of Agriculture and Food, *Annual Review and Outlook 1998*.

TABLE 6.3: Percent of total direct payments to each farm
income group 1992–1997.

	1992	1995	1997	% of 1997 Population
< £2,500	21	6	9	20
£2,500-£5,000	17	9	11	20
£5,000-£10,000	28	16	20	23
£10,000-£15,000	12	17	15	12
£15,000-£20,000	9	11	13	8
£20,000-£30,000	6	16	15	10
> £30,000	7	25	16	7
All	100	100	100	100

Source: NFS.

prices by the introduction of a dairy cow premium (as is proposed for the middle of the next decade in the May 1999 Berlin Agreement) then the distribution of direct payments will come to resemble much more closely the distribution of farm income itself. Under current policies, we will get closer to the situation where the top-earning 20 per cent of farms will attract 60 per cent of the direct payments.

TABLE 6.4: Concentration coefficients for specified direct
payment schemes.

Components	1992	1996
Arable aid	n.a.	.5891
Suckler cow premium	n.a.	.1449
Special beef premium	n.a.	.3752
Cross compliance schemes[1]	n.a.	.2568
Pre1992 schemes[2]	.2226	.1829
Sundry[3]	n.a.	.4123
Market-based income	.7960	.9241
Total	.6277	.5475

1 Cross compliance schemes include those where farmers have to comply with
environmental restrictions to qualify for payment. They include the Extensification Premium and REPS payments.
2 Pre-1992 schemes include the Disadvantaged Area Scheme and the Ewe
Premium.
3 Sundry schemes include schemes not classified elsewhere.
Source: Keeney, M., 'The distributional effects of direct payments on Irish
farm unions', *Journal of Agricultural Economics*, forthcoming.

Which support schemes are the most targeted?

An interesting question to ask of the distributional impact of
farm support schemes is whether one scheme might be preferred
over another purely on the grounds of its distributional impact.
The distributional impact of individual schemes can be sum-
marised by an indicator called its *concentration coefficient*. This
coefficient takes a value between 0 and 1, with values closer to
0 indicating a more equal distribution of benefits and values
closer to 1 indicating a more unequal distribution of benefits.

Table 6.4 shows concentration coefficients calculated for
various support schemes as well as for market-based income.
Market-based income is defined as family farm income less
direct payments, and we have already seen that this is negative
on more than 30 per cent of farms. The concentration coefficient for market-based income is thus very close to 1, indicating that this type of income is very concentrated on the highest-
earning farms.

With the exception of the arable aid scheme, all direct payment schemes have a concentration coefficient which is less

than the concentration coefficient for total income.[9] This means that most direct payment schemes contribute to making total income less unequal. The arable aid scheme is the exception and its concentration coefficient indicates that better-off farms benefit disproportionately from the arable hectare payments. The Suckler Cow Premium turns out to be the scheme which is most equally distributed among farms ranked in total income terms. Headage payments under the Disadvantaged Areas Scheme also turn out to be well targetted on low-income farms. It is these schemes which should be favoured if agricultural policy wants to address the needs of low-income farmers.

The extent of farm poverty

Given the heterogeneity of farm incomes, the key concern in incomes policy should be not so much the average income level of farmers but rather the proportion of farmers who fall below a particular income level and live in poverty. Has the massive transfer of resources to agriculture succeeded in eliminating poverty among farmers? Is poverty more likely among farmers than among other groups in society? How important is farm poverty relative to overall poverty in Ireland?

Although the concept of poverty is relatively straightforward, relating as it does to the exclusion from ordinary life due to lack of resources, its measurement is more problematic. Where do we draw the poverty line? What should be the unit of observation? These issues have been extensively explored by the poverty research programme at the Economic and Social Research Institute, Dublin. Poverty analysis has relied on income data from the Household Budget Survey in the past, and more recently has drawn on the 1994 and 1997 Living in Ireland Surveys. The survey units are households, and thus the observations are of the total income of farm households and not just income from farming or the income of the farmer alone. From a poverty perspective, this is clearly the relevant measure, but it means that the data are not comparable with those presented in the farm income distributions in the previous section.

The ESRI researchers suggest the use of a relative income poverty line set at either 50 or 60 per cent of average household income, taking differences in household size and composition into account. Such differences are typically treated through the use of equivalence scales or what EUROSTAT calls consumer units (e.g. the household head is given a value of 1, other adults 0.66, children 0.33). For an adult living alone, this produced poverty lines in 1994 of about £65 and £77 per week, and in 1997 £80 and £96 per week.

In looking at the importance of farm poverty, two concepts are usually used, namely, the risk and incidence of poverty (a third concept – that of the *severity* of poverty – might also be mentioned which refers to how far incomes are below the poverty line). The risk of poverty is the probability of being poor for those belonging to a particular group. This indicator indicates which people in society are most likely to be poor. Even if a group has a high risk of poverty, it might still account for a relatively small proportion of the total numbers in poverty if the group formed only a small proportion of the population. The incidence of poverty is the percentage of all poor households or persons who belong to a certain group or category. Thus one might have a situation where 50 per cent of a certain group of households were poor (risk) but they only comprised 5 per cent of all poor households (incidence). This would happen because they only formed a small percentage of the total population.

The risk of a farm household being classified as poor (measured at the 50 per cent relative income line) is shown in Table 6.5. The figures in the table must be read in conjunction with Figure 1.1 showing aggregate farm income levels in each year. Because of the fluctuations in income from farming from year to year, the proportion of farm households classified as in poverty in any year can be influenced by the timing of the survey.

In 1973, for example, farm incomes were very buoyant because of EU membership and around 20 per cent of households

TABLE 6.5: Risk of poverty by labour force status of head of household (50 per cent relative income poverty line), 1973–97.

Labour force status of household head	1973 HBS	1980 HBS	1987 ESRI	1994 LII	1997 LII
	Percent of total poverty in each group (%)				
Employee	3.9	3.7	3.5	3.1	6.6
Self-employed (excl. farmers)	10.1	8.6	10.5	14.7	20.4
Farmer	21.2	27.0	32.8	20.4	12.5
Unemployed	61.9	63.1	57.2	59.4	60.1
Ill/disabled	42.8	48.2	33.7	44.5	56.5
Retired	29.5	23.3	9.1	10.6	21.3
Home duties	42.2	32.2	9.8	34.9	51.2
Total	18.3	16.8	16.3	18.5	21.9

Sources: Callan, T. et al., *Poverty in the 1990s*, Dublin, Oak Tree Press, 1996; ESRI, *Monitoring Poverty Trends*, Dublin, Stationery Office, 1999.

TABLE 6.6: Composition of households under 50 per cent relative income poverty line by labour force status of head of household, 1973–97.

Labour force status of household head	1973 HBS	1980 HBS	1987 ESRI	1994 LII	1997 LII
	Percent of total poverty in each group (%)				
Employee	9.0	10.3	8.2	6.2	12.7
Self-employed (excl. farmers)	3.6	3.5	4.8	6.7	7.7
Farmer	26.0	25.9	23.7	8.9	3.8
Unemployed	9.6	14.7	37.4	32.6	21.1
Ill/disabled	10.2	9.3	11.1	9.5	9.8
Retired	17.0	18.9	8.1	10.5	15.7
Home duties	24.6	17.4	6.7	23.5	28.9
Total	100.0	100.0	100.0	100.0	100.0

Sources: Callan, T. et al., *Poverty in the 1990s*, Dublin, Oak Tree Press, 1996; ESRI, *Monitoring Poverty Trends*, Dublin, Stationery Office, 1999.

were classified as falling below the poverty line. The incomes included in the 1987 survey were those reported in 1986, which Figure 1.2 has shown was a dreadful year for farm income and the proportion in poverty rose to one-third of all farm households. By 1994 (based on 1993 farm incomes) the proportion had fallen back to 20 per cent, and in the most recent 1997 survey (based on 1996 farm incomes) the proportion was even lower, at

12.5 per cent of farm households. (The risk figures for the 60 per cent relative income line in 1994 and 1997 were 32.2 and 27.3 per cent, respectively). Comparison with other groups in the table shows that unemployed households have the greatest risk of being in poverty, with a consistent proportion around 60 per cent classified as poor. Overall, around 22 per cent of households were classified as poor in the 1997 survey. This represents an increase from 18.5 per cent over the previous four years and reflects the unequal distribution of the benefits of the Celtic Tiger boom. The figures emphasise, however, that fewer farm households were at risk of being poor than in the state as a whole.

The declining risk of poverty among farm households in recent years is reflected even more strongly in the declining share of farm households among all households classified as poor. In the 1970s and 1980s farm households consistently made up 25 per cent of all poor households; by 1997 this proportion had declined to less than 4 per cent (it was only slightly higher, at 5.3 per cent, if the 60 per cent relative income line is used). The objection might be raised that the 1997 figures show farm household incomes in an unusually favourable light, for the same reasons that the 1987 survey showed them in an unusually unfavourable light. Aggregate income from farming peaked in 1996 and has fallen in both 1997 and 1998. It might be reasonable to assume that the incidence of farm poverty has increased again as a result. On the other hand, there are a number of reasons to believe that the disappearance of farm poverty as a significant component of the (growing) Irish poverty problem represents a more permanent change.

First, farm households make up a declining share of the total population, down from 22 per cent in 1973 to less than 8 per cent in 1997. Even if the risk of poverty among farm households remained the same, this alone would lead to a reduction in the incidence of farm poverty. Second, the importance of income from farming in the total income of farm households has also diminished. We saw in the last chapter that only one-half of total farm household income is now derived from farming. As a result, total household income is now less influenced by fluctuations in income from farming. Third, the introduction of a contributory social welfare pension for farmers over sixty-seven (as noted, up to 20 per cent of those defined as farmers are over this age) has directed assistance to a particularly vulnerable group.

It is recognised widely that reliance on income alone is not necessarily a good measure of low consumption and therefore of deprivation. ESRI researchers have provided a definition of *basic deprivation* comprising a set of eight indicators, for example, the enforced absence of such items as food, clothing and heat or going into debt to meet ordinary living expenses. A combined income and deprivation standard can be constructed which defines a household as poor where it reports an enforced lack of at least one of these basic items *and* falls below 60 per cent of mean income. ESRI researchers feel that this combined measure best captures the underlying conceptualisation of poverty as involving enforced absence of socially defined necessities.

An analysis of the 1994 LII survey was conducted by type of area in which one of the areas defined was 'open country'. Over 37 per cent of all households in the state lived in this type of area, so these households clearly embrace many more households than simply farm households, though all farm households will be counted in this category. It is thus interesting that whereas the 1994 survey found that 20 per cent of these households fell below the 50 per cent relative income poverty line (exactly the same proportion as for those households with some farm income), less than 10 per cent were defined as poor on the combined income and deprivation standard (the corresponding figures for the state as a whole were 19 and 15 per cent). We can conclude from this analysis that an income poverty line appears to overestimate the risk of poverty for farm households while underestimating it particularly for households in the Dublin area. One explanation for this might be that farm household income simply 'goes further' than income accruing to other households. This might be either because the cost of living is lower in rural areas or because virtually all farmers live in their own houses and thus benefit from lower housing outlays than other households. Thus the 1994 figure that less than 5 per cent of all poor households are farm households may not be too far off the mark even in the more difficult farming circumstances of 1998.

Addressing low farm incomes

While low-income farm households now make up a very small proportion of all households in poverty, their needs must not be overlooked. These are small farmers, many of them elderly, with a low level of educational attainment and a relatively high proportion of direct payments as a proportion of their income. Their needs will hardly be addressed through agricultural policy and the recently announced Farm Assist Scheme is a better approach to their specific problems. This scheme subsumed the previous Smallholders Unemployment Assistance scheme from April 1999. The new system provides for changes in assessing the means of families applying for the Smallholders Assistance. Income disregards for children are introduced, and only 80 per cent of remaining farm income is counted for the purpose of the means test.

These changes mean that many farm families who do not currently qualify for assistance will qualify under the new arrangements, and many families who currently qualify will be eligible for higher rates of payment. The number of families benefiting is expected to double, from 6,800 to 13,600. The new allowance will be paid to farmers who are aged between eighteen and sixty-six years. It is estimated that the scheme will cost around £48 in a full year compared to the existing smallholders scheme which cost £33 million in 1998. It is salutary to compare the £48 million directed to alleviating the specific problem of farm poverty with the £1 billion given to farmers in general in direct payments and the £2.6 billion cost of providing all supports to agriculture. What additional benefits does society get from these huge disparities? Do we place such a high value on the environmental benefits of modern farming and keeping more people on the land? These questions are rarely asked because it is believed that to question the existing agricultural policy would jeopardise the sizeable transfers which Irelamd receives under the CAP. The next chapter argues that Ireland as a whole would not necessarily lose out from a reform of the CAP. If agricultural policy reform makes sense, we should not be inhibited from pursuing it because of the fear of losing the EU transfers.

7. Ireland's interest in CAP reform

The case for reform of agricultural policy is a strong one at EU level, but should Ireland go along with this? Farmers' interest in continuing the present policy is an obvious one, but what about the wider national interest? Does it benefit Irish society as a whole to defend the current levels of protection under the Common Agricultural Policy?

Farmers argue that what is good for farming is good for the whole economy, and point to the substantial EU receipts which result from the present CAP. In Chapter 4 these were estimated at £1.7 billion in 1997 or around 4 per cent of GNP. If farm protection were eliminated, much of these transfers would disappear. Surely Ireland as a whole would lose out from such a policy change?

On the other hand, earlier chapters have pointed to the huge cost of making these transfers to agriculture and to the production inefficiency induced by the present policy. The volume of Irish agricultural output is now essentially quota-constrained so these inefficiencies will increase over time. It is an empirical question whether the transfer costs and production inefficiencies outweigh the value of the support received from Europe, and whether Irish society would gain from a less protectionist CAP.

This chapter sets out an approach to thinking about the alternative of life without the present CAP. It defines for the first time a new measure of agriculture's contribution to national income. It compares this contribution both under the present CAP regime and what it could be under alternative, less protectionist, scenarios. Such comparisons are inevitably hedged about with huge uncertainty because of the magnitude of the change contemplated. Even the value of formal modelling is limited because a change to world market prices for food within Europe is outside the range of previous experience. Despite the informal approach to comparisons in this chapter, there is a range of feasible scenarios which could both eliminate market price support and ensure that the economy as a whole would be better off than at present. This argument is supported by a brief examination of New Zealand's liberalisation experience in the 1980s when agricultural support there was eliminated. While its experience would not necessarily be automatically replicated elsewhere, there are important lessons to be learned from it.

Agriculture's economic contribution

Return to the income account showing the relationship between measures of farm income in Table 1.1. In this table, net value added at market prices was defined as the difference between the value of farm output measured at market prices, on the one hand, and the value of materials and service inputs and depreciation, on the other hand. Net value added measured at market prices would normally be taken as an indicator of a sector's contribution to the overall economy. However, this indicator both under-estimates and over-estimates the importance of agriculture. It under-estimates the contribution of farming because measuring value added at market prices ignores the value of production-linked EU subsidies attracted to the Irish economy by producing agricultural products. On the other hand, it over-estimates the economic contribution of farming by ignoring the fact that some of the value added at market prices is contributed by Irish consumers who are forced to pay higher prices as a result of CAP protectionism. It also ignores the fact that the Irish taxpayer pays for some of these subsidies either directly (through co-financing of some EU direct payment schemes) or indirectly (through Ireland's contribution to the cost of financing EU subsidies). Thus we develop a measure of agriculture's economic contribution which nets out these internal transfers in order to give a 'pure' measure of the sector's contribution to the Irish economy.

Table 7.1 presents the calculation of agriculture's economic contribution in 1997, a normal year in terms of aggregate income from farming (see Fig. 1.1). In order to include the value of EU production-linked payments, the calculation begins by adding the value of subsidies (less levies) to net value added at market prices to get net value added at factor cost.[10] From this we subtract the purely national transfers to farming from Irish consumers and taxpayers. The resulting net figure is defined as agriculture's economic contribution to Irish society. It is a measure of how much worse off Irish society would be if farming ceased in the morning. It is a good deal less than the usual measure of agricultural value added because it recognises that, from a national point of view, some of the apparent value added in farming is offset by equivalent losses to Irish consumers and taxpayers. By pure coincidence, the value of subsidies in 1997 almost exactly equalled the cost of the transfer to farmers from Irish taxpayers and consumers, so that agriculture's economic contribution is very close to net value added at market prices. However, there is no rule that these two indicators should be similar and they could be quite different in other years.

This is the first time a true measure of agriculture's economic contribution has been calculated. There are two possible criticisms of the measure. First, it ignores the possible multiplier effects of agricultural activity in generating income and employment in upstream and downstream industries. Generally, the multiplier[11] is one of the most abused economic concepts and has very little validity in a time of nearly-full employment. However, to the extent that some sectors of the food industry depend on processing Irish agricultural raw materials, their

TABLE 7.1: Agriculture's economic contribution in 1997 and under alternative future scenarios.

	1997 values	Free trade + no direct payments		Free trade + partial direct payments		Free trade + existing direct payments	
	£m	£m	change over 1997(%)	£m	change over 1997(%)	£m	change over 1997(%)
	(1)	(2)	(3)	(4)	(5)	(6)	(7)
GAO at market prices	3,315	2,210	33	2,210	33	2,210	33
Value of materials and services inputs	1,650						
Depreciation	436						
Total inputs	2,086	984	53	1,399	33	1,767	15
NVA at market prices	1,229	1,226		811	34	443	64
Subsidies less levies	917	0		500		917	
NVA at factor cost	2,146	1,226	43	1,311	39	1,360	37
Less contribution of Irish taxpayer	438	0		85		134	
Less contribution of Irish consumer	482	0		0		0	
Agriculture's economic contribution	1,226	1,226	0	1,226	0	1,226	0
GAO + DPs (value of farm revenue)	4,232	2,210		2,710		3,127	
Inputs to revenue ratio (%)	49	45		52		57	

Source: As described in the text.

value added could be added to agriculture's economic contribution to arrive at an overall contribution of the agri-food sector. This relationship with the food industry will be examined later in the context of the scenario modelling.

A second criticism is that the procedure ignores any benefits of agricultural production to Irish society that are not reflected in the value of food production. Two external benefits which might be overlooked in this process are environmental benefits and rural development benefits. Environmental benefits are recognised to the extent that the subsidies include around £100 million paid through the Rural Environment Protection Scheme to farmers. However, if the public's valuation of landscape benefits are higher than this, then this excess should be credited to agriculture's economic contribution. Similarly, if the public places a higher value on economic activity in rural areas than economic activity in general, then value added in agriculture should be weighted proportionately higher to reflect this. Payments to farmers in disadvantaged areas which are already included in the subsidies figure at least partly recognise this fact.

Now we consider what agriculture's contribution might be in a free trade situation. The significance of free trade is that market price support is eliminated. Three scenarios are considered. The first – and most dramatic – from Ireland's point of view is that the EU moves to free trade in agricultural products *and* removes all direct payments as well. The second scenario is one that allows for free trade and the maintenance of direct payments for environmental purposes and for conserving farming in less favoured regions.[12] We assume, in line with EU policy to place more emphasis on the environment, that these payments are increased to £500m with a national contribution of £100m. The third and most favourable scenario combines free trade with the maintenance of direct payments to farmers at their current level of around £940m of which the Irish contribution would be around £135m.[13] We assume that these are paid as area payments for environmental and rural development purposes. Note that in this last scenario that the EU agricultural budget still drops by one half, so that there would be substantial budget savings to the EU.

To complete the scenarios, we need to consider the likely drop in Irish farm prices under free trade and the supply response of farmers to that reduction. The earlier discussion of the relationship between Irish farm prices and world prices suggested a price gap of around 50 per cent on average across all farm commodities. Removing this price gap would lead to a 33 per cent fall in Irish farm prices. Despite the size of this fall in *price*, there are good grounds for believing that the *volume* of farm output would remain unaltered.

This assumption can be defended on two grounds. The first is that empirical estimates of the aggregate supply elasticity for farm produce are usually quite low. More importantly, the current level of Irish agricultural output is heavily restricted by quotas. These include milk quotas, arable land set aside and individual premium ceilings on sheep and beef herds. Where these quotas are severe, as in the case of milk production, it is even possible that production would expand at the lower price when quotas are removed.

This was the conclusion of a modelling exercise conducted by the Food and Agricultural Policy Research Institute in a recent examination of the effect of removing dairy quotas and intervention support in the EU without compensation. In the first year after quotas and intervention-buying are eliminated, milk prices fall by 20 per cent and milk production increases by 5 per cent, relative to a continuation of the current milk support arrangements. In the longer run, milk prices fall by 27 per cent and production increases by 8 per cent.[14] Note that the long-run fall in milk prices is of a similar order of magnitude to that assumed above, and yet production is projected to increase. Some of the increased milk production would be at the expense of competing enterprises and therefore aggregate output would not increase by as much. However, if support for competing enterprises was also removed at the same time, the increase in milk production would be even greater.

There is further evidence that Irish farmers would react in a similar manner from a survey of intensive dairy farmers in the South of Ireland undertaken by Shane Roberts of UCD.[15] These farmers were asked how they would respond to the elimination of quotas together with a 25–30 per cent fall in milk prices as projected in the FAPRI study, assuming the prices of all other commodities remained the same. Bearing in mind that these were intensive farmers, the results are nevertheless astonishing. The average *increase* in milk production expected among the farmers surveyed was between 40 and 56 per cent. Most of this increase would come from switching land from lower-value dry-stock production to dairying, little change was foreseen in stocking density in dairying, and yields were expected to increase a little. Given these reactions, the assumption that the overall olume of Irish agricultural output would not change even if average prices fell by 33 per cent seems eminently plausible.

With these assumptions, the three scenarios are developed in Table 7.1 as follows. Rather than trying to predict how inputs would respond to the lower level of prices, it is assumed in each scenario that agriculture's economic contribution remains static. The implications for input use are then explored and the plausibility of each scenario examined.

The most extreme scenario is examined first in column 2. A 33 per cent reduction in average farm prices, assuming no change in the volume of output, means that the value of gross agricultural output at market prices would fall to £2,210m. The requirement that agriculture's economic contribution must remain at £1,226m, and given that there are no transfers from Irish consumers and taxpayers nor any subsidies from the EU, means that the value of factor inputs (net value added at factor cost) would have to fall to £1,226m or by 43 per cent, while the value of inputs would be restricted to £984m, a fall of 53 per cent on the original value. Some of this fall in value would be matched by a fall in input prices, but relatively little. So on the assumption that the volume of output remains unchanged, this would imply an approximate doubling of input productivity in response to the fall in prices. While the current CAP regime is undoubtedly associated with great inefficiencies, a doubling of input productivity in response to lower prices does not appear plausible. So we conclude that agriculture's economic contribution could not be maintained under this scenario and that Ireland as a whole would be worse off if free trade and the elimination of all EU subsidies was the alternative.

The second scenario involves the partial retention of subsidies and is shown in Column 4 of Table 7.1. Using the same reasoning, this suggests that a fall of about one-third in the volume of both material and factor inputs would be required to maintain agriculture's economic contribution at the current level. Given the resource savings which could be achieved by being released from the wasteful practices of the CAP (production ceilings on efficient producers, land set aside, the requirement to produce in order to obtain payments) plus the structural change implied by a one-third reduction in the number of farmers, this level of increase in resource productivity is attainable. Of course, if direct payments could be maintained at their current level, which is the third scenario shown in column 6, the likelihood of maintaining or even increasing agriculture's economic contribution is enhanced.

Concerns about possible negative impacts on the food industry in these scenarios are not warranted, given the assumption that the overall volume of farm output is not affected. Indeed, access to cheaper raw materials would improve the competitiveness of the food industry and would lead to further gains not captured here. The maintenance of production would also secure the environmental benefits associated with farming; indeed, the implied reduction in input use would reduce the negative stresses placed by agriculture on the environment and lead to other gains in national welfare not captured in the table above.

Furthermore, the benefits would cumulate over time. Instead of retaining resources in agriculture in order to capture EU transfers which will be continually under threat and which are bounded in size, we encourage a process of structural adjustment in which rural labour and capital are relocated and employed in industries with buoyant markets and the prospects of expansion and growth. In the longer term, it is a much more secure future for the Irish economy.

The New Zealand experience

In the mid-1980s New Zealand removed all support to farming. In early 1984 the government announced the ending of output-price assistance for agricultural products. Subsequently, fertiliser and other input subsidies were abolished as were investment and land-development concessions. In addition, tax concessions for farmers were withdrawn. Free government services were eliminated. Producer Boards had their access to concessionary

Reserve Bank funding withdrawn; they now have no access to taxpayer funds. Starting in 1987, central government subsidies for soil conservation, flood control and drainage schemes were substantially eliminated, although some transfer payments generated at a local authority level continue to contribute to funding.

It is often believed that New Zealand farmers received little support anyway prior to this dramatic policy change. However, pastoral agriculture in New Zealand benefited from an average PSE of 24 per cent in 1979–86 (this was as high as 34 per cent in 1983, just before the policy change) and compares to the PSE of 45–50 per cent for Irish livestock production. After the policy change the New Zealand PSE dropped to about 4 per cent and it is currently less than 1 per cent. Has New Zealand agriculture collapsed?

Farm incomes did decline during the 1980s, but this fall did not result solely from the removal of government support. A tight macroeconomic policy led to high interest rates and an inflow of capital which brought about an appreciation of the exchange rate. This caused more damage to New Zealand farming than the removal of support. From 1988 on, farm prices improved and farmers' terms of exchange strengthened both as a result of the reforms and improving world market prices for pastoral commodities. Eventually, farmers also benefited from falling input prices and from lower processing costs.

New Zealand farmers have proved remarkably resilient in adapting to the changes that have swept the sector. Operating expenses, as a percentage of gross farm income, fell from a peak of 80 per cent in 1984 to about 50 per cent currently. This is relevant to the projected reaction in Ireland to lower prices resulting from a move to free trade in the three scenarios above. Thus, increased operating efficiency, and the removal of protection from input industries, helped farmers cope with the decline in prices. Very few farmers were forced by the reforms to leave the land. Statistics suggest that total farm numbers have actually increased after the policy reform. The rural collapse predicted by some never happened. New Zealand's rural population rose slightly between the 1981 census and the 1991 census despite the removal of subsidies. The rural economy has become more diversified, with tourism and other services accounting for a larger share of rural economic activity. This diversification has made rural communities less vulnerable to cyclical downturns in the agricultural sector.

Conclusions

Ireland is unique among EU member states in having by far the highest transfers in proportion to GNP arising from the operation of the CAP. They amounted to about 4 per cent of GNP in 1997. Farmers have used these transfers to argue in favour of the *status quo* and in defence of the CAP. The burdens placed on Irish consumers and taxpayers to pay for farm support are justified by the even larger transfers from Europe.

Transfers made, however, are not the same as benefits received. While there are always costs associated with making transfers, the costs of farm transfers under the Common Agricultural Policy are particularly large. They are of two main kinds. The first are the costs associated with making the transfer. These include both operating costs (for example, associated with intervention) and leakages (particularly to third countries). The second are the costs associated with the rules for receiving the transfers. As a result of these rules (quota restrictions on production, land set aside, the requirement to produce in order to be eligible for payment), the costs of producing the current level of Irish agricultural output are much higher than they need to be. It is not unreasonable to suggest that the same level of output could be produced with a third less resources than are currently used if more optimal farm structures were in place. Once both sets of costs are deducted from the value of the transfers, the benefits of the current CAP arrangements are much less clear-cut.

The chapter develops for the first time a measure of agriculture's economic contribution to Irish society. From a national perspective, it is this measure which should be used to evaluate the net benefits and costs of alternative agricultural policy scenarios. The results of some informal scenario modelling suggest that national policy options are more open than has been recognised heretofore. Irish society would lose out if the EU moved to free trade in agriculture and if, at the same time, it eliminated all direct payment programmes. But while the elimination of market price support should be welcomed, there is no reason to believe that the EU would want to eliminate all budgetary support to farmers. In fact, direct payments to farmers for agri-environment and rural development purposes are strongly favoured in Brussels. This chapter has argued that the Irish economy would be at least as well off following the removal of market price support under the CAP-provided EU direct payments continued at between 50–100 per cent of their present levels. Given this finding, it is no longer necessarily in the interests of Irish society as a whole to defend the continuation of market price support if, by so doing, it places other interests in jeopardy.

8. Reform of farm income support

Since the 1930s, it has been an aim of public policy to transfer income to the farming community. Until EU membership in 1973, the state's ability to pursue this aim was limited both by the relative size of the farming sector in the total population (even in 1973, farmers made up 22 per cent of the labour force) and by its low level of economic development. EU membership changed the rules fundamentally. Following EU membership, support to farmers took a quantum leap until today it accounts for the entire aggregate income from farming.

At first sight, the policy looks like a remarkably successful one. There is no longer a generalised farm-income problem in Ireland today. The return to labour employed in agriculture still falls below average industrial earnings, but this reflects remaining differences in age and education levels between the farm and non-farm workforces and is not a characteristic of agricultural production as such. In fact, the total income of farm households now exceeds average household income in the state. The quality of the rural housing stock which was in a pitiable condition in the 1960s has been transformed out of all recognition. The risk of poverty among farmers has fallen dramatically and the proportion of poor households headed by a farmer is now less than 5 per cent of all poor households in the state. Occasional income crises caused by fluctuations in farm prices or weather conditions continue to occur, but this problem needs to be addressed by better risk-management facilities and insurance schemes, not by further generalised income transfers.

It is wrong, however, to jump to conclusions based purely on the coincidence of events. The massive support to farming has helped to raise incomes from farming – it would be hard for it not to have had any effect! – but other factors have been at work as well. Structural changes in farming which have led to higher productivity and a declining agricultural workforce are obviously a key factor. These changes have been facilitated by the growing propensity of members of the farm household – either the farmer himself or herself or his or her spouse – to work off the farm. Almost half of all farm households now have income from off-farm employment. The availability of employment in rural areas, by creating alternative income opportunities, has put a floor under farm incomes. Without farm support, there would be fewer farmers, but it is unlikely that they would work for a lower income. Linked to this has been a rising educational level, particularly among younger farmers. A principal reason for low farm incomes in the past was the low level of educational attainment among farmers. Longer schooling not only opens more off-farm opportunities but also improves farm performance. Finally, given that over one-fifth of farmers are over sixty-five years of age, improvements in social welfare pensions have helped to raise incomes among elderly farmers.

Furthermore, income-support policy under the CAP is neither particularly efficient nor effective. Market support policies, in particular, are costly to implement. Overall, we estimate that one-third of the value of EU transfers are dissipated before they reach the farmers they are intended to benefit. In the beef sector, probably half of the transfers from taxpayers and consumers are swallowed up by the costs of intervention, by the rents extracted by the meat processors and by the terms of trade gains to third-country purchasers of beef.

A key finding of this book is that the resources employed in farming are producing little real value added when measured at world market prices. The entire income from farming is due to public support. The farming industry has become a gigantic social welfare client. Surely it is ludicrous that farmers must produce at a loss (measured at market prices) simply to qualify for direct payments. The waste of resources is colossal but it is just one example of the many inefficiencies inherent in the present system of farm support.

Income support policies are also poorly targeted. In Ireland, around 60 per cent of the total support goes to the top-earning 20 per cent of farms. Around 146 farmers get over £100,000 each in direct payments annually. It is hard to believe that this money is needed to prevent them falling into poverty, or that their contribution to a vibrant rural society is so much greater than the average farmer's. If the object is to raise farmers' living standards to the society's average or to maintain the number of farm families by ensuring a minimum income level then this funding is simply misdirected. As the effect of market price support policies is equivalent to placing a 20 per cent VAT tax on food, the redistribution of income is particularly perverse.

Most of the benefits of price support are ultimately capitalised into the value of land. This is clearly indicated by the sky-high prices paid for agricultural land particularly where there are quota or premium rights attached. In Ireland, where most farmers are owner-occupiers and where land is mainly transferred through inheritance, this makes little difference to farm incomes.

However, those farmers who need to rent additional acres or to buy extra land will be well aware that the benefits of price support are captured by the land-owner and not by the farmer.

Challenges to the CAP

Critics and sceptics have forecast the demise of agricultural protectionism for many years. The CAP has certainly changed its shape, most notably as a result of the MacSharry reforms, but support to farmers continues unabated. The Agenda 2000 negotiations were the most recent attempt to forge an EU agricultural strategy forward to the middle of the next decade. The purpose of these negotiations was to make possible the next enlargement of the EU to accommodate the countries of central and eastern Europe, as well as to prepare the EU for the forthcoming Millenium Round of WTO trade negotiations. Agreement was reached to take another step along the road of substituting direct payments for market price support, but with such generous compensation that Irish farmers emerged better off by over £400 million over the seven-year period after the negotiations. As the Agenda 2000 package covers the period from 2000 to 2006, the future of the CAP would appear secure for some time to come.

However, the negotiators agreed that the Agenda 2000 agreement could be reviewed after 2002 if the need arose. Indeed, many commentators believe that the Agenda 2000 reforms were not ambitious enough to prepare for the challenges ahead and that the agreement will have to be reviewed. Among the drivers of change will be the EU enlargement to eastern Europe and the forthcoming Millenium Round of WTO world trade negotiations.

The EU's eastern enlargement will significantly extend both the union's agricultural capacity and its number of farmers. It will be a costly affair to extend the existing CAP with its protected prices and direct payments. The commission has thus stated that the new member states should not expect to benefit from the compensatory direct payments which are paid to farmers in the existing EU. It seems hardly credible that the EU can continue to make huge area payments to cereal farmers in the former East Germany, while across the border in the Czech Republic farmers will be denied these payments. It hardly reflects the spirit of the single market. While the date of accession for the eastern applicants is still undetermined and it may not take place within the framework of the current Agenda 2000 agreement on EU finances, in the longer run the EU must either accept that enlargement will be more expensive than it has hitherto admitted or the CAP itself must be changed to accommodate the enlargement process.

Direct payments and export subsidies will also be targets in the forthcoming WTO Millenium trade talks. While the WTO does not object to countries providing income support to their farmers, it does insist that this support should be provided in ways which are not trade-distorting. In technical terms, it wants to decouple support from production so that farmers are not encouraged to over-produce and create problems for the world market as a result of farm support policies. However, most EU direct payments are not decoupled. It was only because of a special deal which the EU made with the US at the end of the Uruguay Round of agricultural negotiations that EU direct payments are excluded from the disciplines of support reduction. In 2003, the so-called 'peace clause' which prevents these payments being challenged will lapse and even without further concessions in the Millenium Round, the EU could come under pressure to reform its support system. Export subsidies, which are crucial to the EU's market support policy, will also be challenged by other exporters whose markets are attacked in this way.

A strategy for change

The message of this book is that there is no longer any reason why the non-farm sector should be held to ransom by the farming sector in determining future agricultural policy. Irish taxpayers and consumers currently pay around £900 million annually to farmers through national co-financing of EU schemes, through higher food prices and through the CAP's share of the Irish contribution to the EU budget. Payment of these transfers has been rationalised, partly by an appeal to social solidarity on behalf of a relatively low-income social group, and partly on the grounds that these transfers represent a down-payment which attracted a much larger EU transfer which, in turn, benefited the whole economy.

The argument in this book is that these arguments are no longer persuasive. Farm household incomes now exceed average household incomes in the state, and the risk of poverty among farm families is now much lower than the average for all households. While agricultural support has helped to bring about this situation, agricultural restructuring, the more widespread availability of rural employment, higher educational levels and more generous social welfare assistance have played more important roles. Furthermore, although EU transfers through the agricultural sector amount to about 4 per cent of Irish GNP, the market price support element of this support is transferred so inefficiently and creates such production distortions in the agricultural economy that, as a society, we would be better off without it. It is time for Irish society to adopt a new strategy towards agricultural policy in the EU.

This strategy should consist of three components:

1. the winding-down over a phased and pre-announced period of all EU price support to farming and its substitution by 'national envelopes' containing decoupled payments for support to adjustment assistance and greater emphasis on agri-environment and rural development policies;

2. appropriate risk management and income insurance schemes to protect against severe downturns in farm incomes such as farmers experienced in 1998 and 1999;

3. an intensified rural development strategy designed to strengthen the network of urban towns and villages in rural areas and to increase the availability of off-farm employment opportunities to ensure the viability of rural areas.

The first element of this strategy would target the elimination of market price support while maintaining and expanding direct payment support to farmers (decoupled from production) for social, environmental and rural development reasons. It would be fully in tune with the current EU emphasis on the multifunctionality of agriculture. In practical terms, it would mean that Ireland should signal its intention to join the 'like-minded' group of EU member states, including the UK, Italy and some of the Scandinavian countries, which have been pressing for a more radical CAP reform. The possibility of a further CAP review in 2002 provides a focus to build alliances and to mobilise support for change.

The second element of the strategy recognises the volatility of farm incomes and that there are years when agriculture faces a temporary income crisis. Because most political lobbying goes into seeking to raise the level of farm prices, little attention has been given to ways of offsetting their instability. There is need for new thinking at both the EU and national levels to develop mechanisms to lower or to shift income risk from producers. Possible ideas include more efficient use of taxation arrangements, the greater use of futures markets by farmers and income insurance schemes, if necessary underwritten by public subsidy.

The third element of the strategy is designed to ensure that the inevitable fall in farm numbers in moving to farming at world market prices will not have an adverse impact on rural population and viability. Many good ideas on rural development strategy have been advanced by groups such as the Western Development Commission and are included in the recent White Paper on Rural Development and the National Development Plan. Until now, however, rural development has been completely overshadowed by agricultural policy and the latter has cannabilised resources which could have been used to better effect for rural development objectives. The abandonment of agricultural protection would release much greater energy and resources to more vigorously pursue this goal.

To implement this strategy will require re-organised administrative arrangements. In the centenary year of the Department of Agriculture, Food and Rural Development which was first established in 1900, it is appropriate to ask if this department has now outlived its usefulness. Similar questions are being asked in the UK of their Ministry of Agriculture. The Irish Department of Agriculture has some of the most resourceful and competent civil servants in the entire public service. Their skills have been honed in many late-night battles in Brussels, seeking to nudge yet another concession to Irish farming out of their partners. One measure of their abilities is the way in which a potential £260 million loss to farmers in the original Agenda 2000 proposals was turned into a positive gain by the time the negotiations were completed.

But a separate Department of Agriculture carries the danger that farmers' interests are over-represented in decision-making to the detriment of the national interest. The department (and the minister) measures its success by the level of farm income, not by the size of agriculture's contribution to the national economy. While the farming interest must be given its due weight, a better mechanism needs to be found of weighing its interests against those of the wider economy. This would best be achieved by assigning responsibility for agriculture as an industry to the Department of Enterprise and Employment. Other functions now undertaken by the Department of Agriculture could be assigned to other government departments. For example, agricultural training could be transferred to the Department of Education, rural development would fit appropriately with the Department of the Environment, and payments to farmers could be handled by the Department of Social, Community and Family Affairs. Such a change would clearly signal that agriculture in future would be treated on the same basis as any other sector in the economy. That is the basis for a productive future both for farming and society as a whole.

Notes

1   The O'Connor figures only apply to the seven commodities considered. The OECD methodology for calculating Producer Support Estimates is to 'gross up' the support calculated for the individual commodities they consider to cover total agricultural output, on the assumption that the average support for the commodities not explicitly considered equals the average support for the commodities explicitly considered. This procedure is not followed here because it is considered it would give biased results. However, this implicit assumption that the excluded commodities receive no support will bias the O'Connor estimates downwards in the opposite direction to her use of the OECD reference prices.

2   Under the milk quota regime, each dairy farmer is assigned a milk quota which determines how much milk he or she can sell in any year (the milk quota year runs from April to March). If Irish milk production in any year exceeds the national milk quota (this is simply the sum of all the individual farm-level quotas), then those farmers who are over-quota must pay a fine. Farmers who possess a milk quota but who no longer wish to produce milk can lease or sell their quota to another farmer. The rules governing the transfer of quota between farmers are complex and change from time to time.

3   It is easy to show this because the unit size of export subsidies is much greater than the world price gap used in calculating the trade effect. The difference is the amount of the subsidy which simply offsets the impact on world prices of support provided by the EU and other countries and provides no net gain to farmers.

4   O'Connor, D., 'The Development of a Set of Irish Agricultural Sector Models for Use in the Analysis of Policy Reform', Ph.D, Department of Economics, Trinity College, Dublin, 1998.

5   If the Irish National Accounts are used to calculate the disparity index, then the agricultural sector is defined to include forestry and fishing. Non-farm income is defined to include the sum of non-agricultural wages, salaries and pensions (including employers' contributions to social insurance) plus the income of independent non-agricultural traders and professional earnings.

6   Eurostat, *Total income of agricultural households – 1995 report*, Luxembourg.

7   Consumer units are derived by adjusting household composition to take account of the different consumption patterns of household heads, other adults and children.

8   The National Farm Survey is published annually by Teagasc, the Irish Agriculture and Food Development Authority. The Household Budget Survey is published by the Central Statistics Office. The results of the Living in Ireland survey carried out by the Economic and Social Research Institute are published in Callan T., et al., *Poverty in the 1990s*, Dublin, Oak Tree Press, 1996.

9   The concentration coefficient for total income is more usually called the Gini coefficient.

10   Some levies are paid to the Irish exchequer rather than to Brussels and should be subtracted from the Irish taxpayer contribution rather than from the subsidies figure, but this does not affect the figure calculated for agriculture's economic contribution.

11   The multiplier refers to the effect whereby an increase in agricultural output induces further increases in output in other industries which either supply inputs to agriculture or process agricultural output. As a result, the overall increase in output in the economuy is a multiple of the initial increase in agricultural output.

12   In 1997 payments under these headings amounted to £350m (£125m for headage payments, £125m in the Suckler Cow Premium and £100m in REPS of which around £85m were funded nationally by the Irish Exchequer).

13   This is calculated on the basis that direct payments accounted for about 50 per cent of CAP spending (FEOGA Guarantee and Guidance expenditure) in 1997, so this proportion of the Irish contribution of £268m in 1997 to the cost of the CAP is taken as the cost of direct payments.

14   FAPRI (Food and Agricultural Policy Institute), *Analysis of European Dairy Policy Options*, University of Missouri, 1999.

15   Roberts, S., 'Integrating the Environment and Intensive Dairy Farming in Ireland in the 21st Century', M.Sc. Environmental policy, University College Dublin, 1999.

Bibliography

Callan, T., Nolan, B., Whelan, B., Whelan, C. and Williams J., *Poverty in the 1990s: Evidence from the 1994 Living in Ireland Survey*, Dublin, Oak Tree Press, 1996.

Department of Agriculture, Food and Rural Development, *Annual Review and Outlook* (annual) (available on the web at http://www.irlgov.ie/daff).

Department of Agriculture, Food and Rural Development, *Compendium of Irish Economic and Agricultural Statistics* (various), (available on the web at http://www.irlgov.ie/daff).

ESRI, *Monitoring Poverty Trends*, Dublin, Stationery Office, 1999.

Eurostat, 1996, *Total Income of Agricultural Households – 1995 Report*, Luxembourg.

Food and Agriculture Policy Research Institute (FAPRI), 1999.

Analysis of European Dairy Policy Options, University of Missouri.

Keeney, M., 1998, 'The distributional effects of direct payments on Irish farm incomes', Teagasc and Trinity College Dublin, mimeo.

Keeney, M., Matthews, A., and Frawley, J., 'The distribution of direct payments in Irish agriculture', Paper read to the Dublin Economics Workshop Conference, Kenmare, 1997.

O'Connor, D., 1998, 'Producer support for the Irish dairy sector in a changing policy environment', Paper presented at a conference on The Future of Irish Dairying: opportunities, constraints and policy, University College Dublin, September 1998.

OECD, *Monitoring and Outlook of Agricultural Policy 1998*, Paris, OECD, 1999.

Roberts, S., 'Integrating the Environment and Intensive Dairy Farming in Ireland in the 21st Century', M.Sc. Environmental Policy thesis, University College Dublin, 1999.

Teagasc, *National Farm Survey* (annual), Dublin, Teagasc.